TALK THERAPY

A Radical History for Troubled Times

Marguerite Valentine
with
Diana Turner, Susan Budnick
& Steve Baker

First published in Great Britain in 2025.

Copyright © Marguerite Valentine 2025, except:
Chapter 14 copyright © Diana Turner 2025;
Chapter 15 copyright © Susan Budnick 2025;
Chapter 18 copyright © Steve Baker 2025.

In memory of those who
lived and worked in an
Arbours Community

Contents

Introduction to 'Talk Therapy'   vii

The Personal is Political

1. Talk Therapy   2
2. Thinking Big: Feeling Small   7
3. A Conversation about Therapy   11

Personal

4. Beginnings   20
5. A Childhood   23
6. The Accident   27
7. Lost in Time and Space   33
8. Rites of Passage—Rum and Blackcurrant   43

And Political

9. Lessons in Disillusionment: London Social Work   50
10. Finding my Self   58
11. The Radical Heart of the Arbours Association   68

Praxis

12. Milieux Therapy in an Arbours Community   82
13. Marguerite on 'Favouritism'   88
14. Diana on 'Knowing and Not Knowing'   100
15. Susan on 'The Mad Tea Party'   110

Thinking and Feeling

16. How can 'Mental Illness' be Understood? 122
17. The Challenge of the Crisis Centre 133
18. Steve on 'Thinking Allowed' 135
19. Marguerite on 'Night Time Terrors' 145

Observing and Interpreting

20. Interpretations: the psychic power of narrative nonfiction 160
21. Film as Clinical Narrative: when the personal becomes political 164
22. Muriel's Wedding: parental failure, female friendship and the cultural significance of weddings 168
23. The Night Porter: the perverse attraction of the 'Bad Object' 175
24. Last Year at Marienbad: the allure of dreaming, the uncertainty of memory, the dread of forgetting 184

Epilogue 192
Biographies 204
Acknowledgements 206

Introduction to 'Talk Therapy'

Consider first Freud's advocacy of psychotherapy as 'the 'talking cure', Rollo Mayo's comment, 'psychotherapy has the potential to set free', or Jung's observation, 'who looks outside, dreams; who looks inside, awakens.' History has proved them right. For those finding life troubling or have been subjected to a diagnosis, medicated, or locked away, the 'talking cure' is both a more compassionate and a more engaged therapy.

The 'therapeutic hour' lasts for fifty minutes, and within that time frame, the emotional history of a patient is explored. Every session holds a possibility that as much or as little in any chapter, in any novel, in any story, can be told. Which is why, for many, analytic psychotherapy never loses its fascination.

The analytic therapist uses no formulas, no techniques, gives no advice, but a body of phenomenological theory informs their work. This develops through dialogue. The patient talks and the therapist listens, and gradually through this process, a pattern is discerned, a history is built, a narrative created. Most often this begins with childhood memories and experiences, which indicate in one way or another why a patient feels and behaves in particular ways. The environment, the regularity, and predictability of sessions is part of this exploration and is fundamental to establishing a safe, psychologically containing place within which therapy can take place. Such details are particularly important for patients who have experienced neglect, confusion, chaos, or trauma in childhood.

'Talk Therapy' is based on the training, the experiences and the politics of a therapeutic organisation called the Arbours Association. Each section whether descriptive or analytic, considers a different facet of therapeutic work, and moves between the strictly personal and the theoretical, with the aim of integrating both perspectives. Along the way aspects such as why consider therapy, who becomes a therapist, and what is milieux therapy, more philosophical issues are also considered. For example, how can mental illness be understood, are Freudian theories still relevant, and is psychotherapy better than medication?

The intention, which is written in the style or perspective of 'narrative nonfiction' or 'genre blending', is to weave into these accounts how analytic psychotherapy works. It does this by contextualising thoughts and experiences as they might occur between the patient and therapist.

Underlying this practice is the idea of the psyche as a concept. Ephemeral, transient, ambiguous, real or imagined, it is comprised of relationships, which understood in its broadest sense thereby includes a past, present and future. The intention being that this not only will inspire a new kind of reflection, but that its reading will be interesting and accessible both for the general reader and the more specialised professional.

The Personal is Political

'Learn to use your life experience in your work. Continually examine and interpret it ... for one thing your past plays into and affects your present, and it defines your capacity for future understanding an experience'

(adapted from *The Sociological Imagination*, 1959, C. Wright Mills)

— CHAPTER 1 —

Talk Therapy

A mental illness is not an illness. It has no agreed set of symptoms; no rash, no temperature, no localised detectable pain, no virus, no bacteria. The most advanced diagnostic medical machine has failed to identify the cause or location of a mental illness. Which is why it might better be understood as a metaphor for a troubled mind or for a sickness of the soul. And, with regard to treatment rather than depending on the questionable power of medication, that we find the possibility of understanding in the words of the poet, the song writer, the novelist, the characters in a film, or arising from within a conversation with a psychotherapist.

This is not a new perspective. From the nineteenth century Freud was aware of the value of psychotherapy. He called these conversations between himself and his patient, the 'talking cure'. And over time he and others came to see their distress as a lived metaphor, a narrative, an experience, a dynamic concept, a chimera, a way of looking at the world, fuelled with phantasy, imagination, anger, cut through with shards of sadness, loss, confusion and yearning. A state of mind which will however require time and understanding to make visible and articulate as a problem of a life.

Yet however identified, still it can be argued that the 'mentally ill' may hold a legitimate view of their world, which is as creative, as perceptive, as expressive, as any protest, even though standing centre stage and in opposition to this alternative, is the 'medical model'. Here the primacy of science with its values of objectivity, certainty and predictability replaces that of the human experience; which is of the particular and the individual. Here conformity rules and nowhere, as evidence, is this more apparent than in the American reference encyclopaedia memorably entitled as *The Diagnostic and Statistical Manual of Mental Disorders* (DSM-5-TR 2022).

Regarded with almost religious fervour by some, if not many in the field of mental illness, its bias is clear; any diagnosis is influenced by and linked to the financial interests of big insurance companies (Vanheule, S. 2014).[1] Hence 'cure' has now become 'commodified and subject to the rules of the market. It is valued, not in terms of any patient's expression of individual creativity and fulfilment, but 'objectively' whereby success is measured and costed in terms of a 'tick box culture'. The consequence? Managers in health centres, hospitals and the universities now hold the financial reins, and it is usually they who make decisions regarding whether a patient is suitable for counselling or psychotherapy or a referral to a psychiatrist.

Given this, it is no surprise the technical and measurable approach of Cognitive Behavioural Therapy (CBT) is favoured above the long term talking therapy of the mid to late twentieth century; which is now likely to be seen as unproven and expensive. And that along with the accompanying notions of treatment, various forms of medication are freely prescribed for depression, anxiety, grief, and confusion, and a management course for anger, (for example) is seen as preferable to understanding why someone feels and behaves out of control.

1 Stijn Vanheule. *Diagnosis and the DSM: A Critical Review.* Palgrave Macmillan, 2014.

The potential to discover individual meaning, to consider the patient's personal history, and in relation to anger, whether words and memories can replace fists, is of little significance. Within this particular consultation, a list of unacceptable behaviour and thoughts is drawn up and replaced by another of more worthy thoughts, to which the patient is urged, with the therapist's support, to adopt. Perhaps the technique works in some cases. But regardless of this, surely such perspectives subtly devalue a patient's narrative, since any understanding or appreciation of a personal story depends upon the ability to listen. Furthermore, it is likely matched by a simultaneous failure to be curious about the meaning of silence or contemplation within a therapeutic session (or anywhere else for that matter).

Thus, the voices of the disaffected are muted by the objections of the opposition. The protests of the repressed, the misunderstood, the poor, the injustice and authoritarianism of the family or of the State is now silenced or ignored. Lost in a miasma of convenience, indifference or denial, mental illness and the practice of psychotherapy have become bureaucratised.

Yet, behind this critique, lies a hidden history, the experience of another way of making sense of the world. Its origins lie in the mid-seventies, when a radically different psychotherapeutic organisation was established. Called the Arbours Association it began in North London and from the start attracted a certain type of savvy professional. Driven by a need to understand why people felt the way they did, and with a desire to enter into a meaningful dialogue, its practitioners sought to establish a different kind of relationship.

Such protests and advocacy for the 'mentally ill' came from the perspectives of the personal, i.e. the philosophical, the progressive sectors of psychiatry, the psychologists, social workers, the academic, the literary, and the filmic. And the fact that then as now, there was no generally accepted scientific explanation for schizophrenia was paradoxically fundamental to developing a different approach in working with disturbance. This alternative and radical perspective which it also should be said, by and large opposed the medical model, depended on an understanding of power.

Power exists, then and now, in each and every relationship, from the party politics of Parliament down to the interactive cameos of family life. Power matters; and it is at its most virulent when it is unseen. A benign force for the good as well as for the bad, its potential to define a situation, lies in its capacity to control, exploit, distort, destroy, as well as develop and protect. So the originality of the Arbours trained psychotherapist lay not only in a critical attitude towards the 'medical model' but also the recognition of the links between the problems of the individual, and important social issues.

Around about the same time, C. Wright Mills' classic book *The Sociological Imagination* (first published in 1959 by Oxford University Press with many later editions up to the present day) was re-published. Written with passion and a keen sense of justice, it was and still is a significant contribution to understanding the problems of society. In a wide ranging critique, the author noted the individual's inability to make the connection between how they feel and large scale changes within the political economy.

On the opening page, he writes, 'Neither the life of the individual nor the history of a society can be understood without both' and the following page contained the premise of the book, '*The Sociological Imagination* enables us to grasp history and biography and the relations between the two within society'.

Such observations would seem appropriate today. Globally the last few years have seen a 25% rise in anxiety, depression, and other mental health issues as reported by WHO.[2] Nearly four million families in the UK now live in destitution.[3] The number of food

---

2   World Health Organization, 'OVID-19 pandemic triggers 25% increase in prevalence of anxiety and depression worldwide', 2 March 2022. https://www.who.int/news/item/02-03-2022-covid-19-pandemic-triggers-25-increase-in-prevalence-of-anxiety-and-depression-worldwide
3   Joseph Rowntree Foundation, *Destitution in the UK, 2023*, 24 October 2023. https://www.jrf.org.uk/deep-poverty-and-destitution/destitution-in-the-uk-2023

banks has risen from 35 in 2010 to 1646 in 2023. The Trussell Trust[4] reports that an estimated 2.99 million emergency food parcels were supplied in 2022/23. Yet there seems a disconnect between the association with the years of austerity following the 2008 crash, to Brexit, and the consequent savage cutbacks to the welfare state. These are ignored. Only the impact of Covid is acknowledged as being significant.

Referring to the recent Global Mind Project, which revealed in a survey of seventy-one similar countries, where the United Kingdom came second from the bottom (only Uzbekistan was worse), George Monbiot in a recent article in *The Guardian* asks why in the UK mental health is deteriorating.[4] Apart from the terminological characteristics of poverty as found in *the Beveridge Report* of 1942 i.e. 'want, disease, ignorance, squalor and idleness' he adds a further category, which is both more relevant and more political.'

Namely, he comments that the previous decades have been marked by environmental chaos, extreme political dysfunction and misrule, impunity for the powerful, and state-sponsored culture wars as a distraction. As a consequence, he writes the political economy has now turned to shit; almost literally in some cases, and that its causes lie in the ideological development of 'neoliberalism' as discussed in his forthcoming book.[5]

As a further response to the social and economic deterioration in people's lives, can be added the observation that the present government seems more concerned to 'create wealth' for a privileged elite. Why else, for example, are banks not taxed on their windfall profits which they enjoy through elevated interest rates and the increasing amount of returns they get through lending to the UK government.[6] Driven by a sense of entitlement rather than compassion and responsibility, it is hardly surprising that parts of the population feel abandoned and despairing.

4 George Monbiot, 'Why is Britain's Mental Health So Incredibly Poor? It's Because Our Society Is Spiralling Backwards'. The Guardian, 10 May 2024.
5 George Monbiot and Peter Hutchison, *The Invisible Doctrine: The Secret History of Neoliberalism (& How It Came to Control Your Life)*. Penguin Books, 2024.
6 Personal Communication Richard Johnson.

— CHAPTER 2 —

Thinking Big: Feeling Small

Whereas C. Wright Mills tended to emphasise the big picture; the State, the economy and the political system, psychotherapists work at the other end of the scale; the individual's attitudes, values, experiences. Both perspectives need the other to get a sense of the totality of what's going on. Psychotherapy is about the minutiae of life. It's about thinking, feeling, seeing, and questioning. The nearest and the neatest description of an analytic therapy is that it's an intuitive overview of life by both therapist and patient. Alternatively, the word 'phenomenological' may be more appropriate, because it is about how a life may be understood and how it might be described in terms of an intense awareness and sensitivity towards patterns of the human experience.

This approach is specific and particular, since it privileges the uniqueness of the individual but also and necessarily touches on universal experiences and dilemmas. Derived from this perspective, which it might be said, is almost Socratic in its search for a truth, the analytic psychotherapist is trained to work with the problems of life. For one thing they have been through a long process of therapy themselves. How else would they understand the profound depths of feeling which may be brought into a consulting room if such feelings are alien to them? They must know within themselves how to access and articulate thoughts and feelings which may sometimes seem on an everyday level, confusing, frightening and unacceptable.

Within the psychotherapeutic session a psychic space in which a dialogue between two people in time blocks of fifty minutes is thus gradually developed. This differs in form, but not content, from milieux therapy as described in Part Four. The timing and the predictability of every session is part of the potential healing and its subject matter can be anything; relationships, trauma, grief, anxiety, depression, fear. Ultimately it's up to the patient, but as all therapists know, any conversation, including the most apparently banal, can, and does, more often than not, lead to something significant; hence the importance of close listening.

Freud in referring to his work as 'talking therapy' observed that all dreams, whether of the day or of the night, lead to the unconscious.[7] Something similar was said centuries earlier by the Romans, who famously but apocryphally noted, all roads lead to Rome; this being what is desired but perhaps unattainable. But however understood, there is something aesthetically pleasing about its metaphoric essence.

At its best, psychotherapy is like a piece of improvised music. The melody may reoccur but either the therapist or the patient may interject with an observation of its originality, its repetition, or its dissonance. At its best, it's a psychic journey with no preconceived stopping or starting points. At its best, its potential is profoundly creative and therapeutic.

Hence, to give a sense of the ambience of a psychotherapeutic session, by using the freedom of real accounts, imagined and actual

---

7 The concept of the unconscious is both complex and controversial, with many doubting, or rejecting its existence. However true or not, it is useful for going some way in providing an 'explanation' for what is not known, for what has been forgotten, for what cannot be thought of, or as a metaphoric place for fears, desires, for forbidden wild phantasies, or as a psychic 'dumping ground' for the horrific nightmares of the night.

dialogue, comments, analysis, and critiques, the intention in *Talk Therapy* is to creatively rise above and beyond the case histories of the didactic textbook. Its aim is to illustrate for the reader the importance of both a personal history and the usefulness of the therapeutic imagination in making sense of some of life's problems.

Thus, the book, which is in one sense is a memoir, illustrates these points. It begins with a chance conversation. Two people, unknown to each other, meet at a party; one diagnosed with depression, the other is a psychotherapist. The conversation illustrates how the therapist might frame a first therapeutic session and how the therapist's growing awareness of loss and trauma points to a possible cause for his depression.

In Part Two, the question is raised; who might choose to become a psychotherapist? What personal issues might have been particularly important in the choice of spending a life analysing why and how? Taking myself as the patient, here I write of my own history. Namely, the consequences of a disrupted childhood, a traumatic road accident, a three month stay on a children's accident ward and the unexplained disappearance of my father who was replaced subsequently and suddenly and without any explanation, by a stepfather. All these experiences were relevant in contributing to a certain mind-set and to my later decision to train as a therapist with the Arbours Association.

The experiences of the Arbours Association, its training and therapeutic work within the Communities and the Crisis Centre, and the fundamental importance of 'milieux therapy' are central to this book. The difficulties, the challenges, the potentially profoundly rewarding experiences of work as a therapist, are discussed, together with a comparison of the very different experiences of three psychotherapy trainees.

In the penultimate section the problems in diagnosing mental illness are critically reviewed. This is followed by a close clinical analysis of challenging 'states of mind'. But rather than considering the written and traditional form of a case history, it is suggested that a film may carry the potential to a greater understanding. As an illustration of this perspective, three iconic films are chosen. Each one is powerful, each one memorable, each one has a history of a critical engagement with different sections of the film-going spectator. This is not by chance. They are powerful works of art and teach something profound about life. The narrative of each chosen film indicates a level of psychological sophistication which is carried through by the brilliance of the actors, the directing, and the cinematography.

The book concludes, as it began, with an imaginary conversation. Set against the 2008 international banking crisis as background, it focuses on how this might be experienced in a very personal and intense way. Consisting of a dialogue between two Crisis Centre psychotherapists, followed by a later individual session with a training psychotherapist, it shows specifically how the political economy interjects into the practice and thinking of psychotherapy. Secondly, how the therapist's interpretation brings together a personal history of the past into the present distress and dilemmas of his patient.

Although the memoir is written in a fairly logical sequence, each section is a 'stand-alone' and can be read in any order, which, it now occurs to me, parallels the experience of being in therapy. In other words, each section contains its own emotional logic, which is the sense of its own beginning and of its own end.

— CHAPTER 3 —

A Conversation about Therapy

So here's the scenario. You're at a party. The music is not too loud, you recognise the music, you even like the music. There's no sign of conflict, everyone is terribly nice, there's no apparent sign of adultery, or of drug taking, and there's the usual numbers of people jammed in the kitchen huddled round the alcohol and the not so exciting food. So far, so predictable. You decide to take a break and sit in the quiet room. You're sitting on the big, squashy, deep blue sofa. It's designed for tall men so it's not particularly built for women, unless they have the stature of an Amazon. So as you sit there silently contemplating the painting on the wall which rather bizarrely depicts a woman with a hat made from a parrot, and just as you're wondering if it's the work of Frida Kahlo, an unknown male enters the room. He's tall, startlingly ordinary, except for the intensity of his gaze.

'Do you mind if I join you?'

You reply that you don't mind at all, but ask if he would close the door behind him.

He sits down on a separate chair and after a minute's silence, he says, 'Do you know the hosts?'

'Yes', you say, 'I know Emily. We're in the same film group. Her partner not so well.'

'Film group?' he says,' not a book group?'

'No, it's a film group. We hire a room upstairs in a pub, watch a film together, and then discuss it.'

He's silent. He looks bemused as if you've told him that you were engaged in some far out, weird, spell-casting ritual, known only to a few. You take a quick glance at him. 'You seem stunned into silence.'

'I am, it's totally new to me. Book groups I've heard of, but not film groups.'

'Life's full of surprises.' He's looking intently at you, so you say, 'You can analyse a film just like characters in a book'. There's no reaction. Your explanation seems to go over his head. You continue, 'I'm wondering what you do for a living … being as a film group seems an alien concept.'

'I'm a software engineer.'

You're momentarily stunned into silence, then you say, 'I have to admit I don't know what that is.'

'I apply engineering and mathematical principles to developing computer programmes.'

'Not much to do with people then.'

'No. I hardly come across them.'

'Well', you say, 'I work with people. I find people interesting, not to say fascinating, a bit like, I'm assuming, you find machines interesting. I want to know why people think and feel the way they do   things like that.'

'That's a big difference. Machines don't feel and I never ask the why of a machine. I ask how.'

'True' you say. 'People aren't machines. People are who they are, because of their early relationships. That's not totally true but it's a start.'

'And your view of AI?'

'Prefer not to engage with that one, at least not right now.'

He's staring at you but then says, 'Are you a psychotherapist?'

'I am a psychotherapist.'

'Really?' His voice rises in surprise.

'Yes, haven't you come across a psychotherapist before? Is it so obvious that's what I do?'

'There's something about you, maybe … I don't know but I have actually … only very recently.' He's briefly silent, then he says, 'I'm depressed, I mean I've got depression, that's what I've been told …' He's looking at you as if expecting you'd say something. He continues, 'The doctor told me I might benefit with some sessions—with a therapist. They have one at the surgery. I've looked it up, what they do. I'd never heard of psychotherapy before. How's it work?'

You feel interested in what he has to say about himself and want to know more, so you don't answer his question straight away. You go sideways on.

'Depression? Okay … But you're also coming across to me as lonely. Are you lonely?'

'I am but how did you know that?'

'It's a guess, from what you've said and how you are … did the doctor also talk about medication, and give you medication?'

'He did, but I'm not a fan. What use is that?'

He looks away as if he wanted to distance himself from the conversation, but he'd already raised your curiosity so you continued. 'But you said he advised "some sessions …" Have you had any sessions yet?'

'Some.'

'And were you assessed, your problem defined, and were you then told how many sessions you would need?'

'Yes. That's about it.'

'So how did you feel about that?'

He shrugs. 'Not much. Too technocratic. Didn't help. What's the point of it all … I'd rather not carry my work style into my personal life. Besides, it's not so straightforward.'

'Being depressed?'

'Yes, depression ... it just happens ... doesn't it?'

'Well, yes and no.'

He glances quickly at you and begins to pick at a loose thread on the arm of his jacket. Was he irritable, bored, or feeling unsettled? You couldn't tell.

'What do you mean?'

'It's complicated ... depression, but what if I told you how I work, as a therapist ... with depression, would you be interested?'

'Maybe. Possibly.'

'Well at the risk of boring you ...'

'I'm not bored. I'm not bored at all.'

'Well, say you'd come to me because ... you couldn't sleep, life seemed pointless, and you felt lonely. I'd ask what's going on for you right now? I'd ask why you chose today out of all days to come and see me?'

'And when I told you, would you write everything down, as I talk?'

'No, I don't take notes, the reason being as well as listening to you, I'm listening to myself in relation to you and thinking about how you affect me.'

'You don't take notes?'

'No, I don't. Taking notes is a distraction ... I'm noticing not only what you say but how you say it, and I'm also noticing if someone gets left out of the story, someone like a father, or someone gets to monopolise your attention, say your mother, or a sibling.' You take a quick look at him. You have his attention, so you continue. 'If possible, and if there's time, because an assessment can stretch over several sessions, I'd go right back into your childhood.' There's a long silence so then you say, 'You seem concerned about my not taking notes.'

He shrugs his shoulders and says, 'It's all too intense.' He's looking at the picture of the woman on the wall across the room.

'Maybe it does sound intense, but that's how it is. Life can be complicated.'

Another silence, this time shorter and then he asks, 'Have you heard of the unconscious?'

If he said this to catch you out, it didn't work, because you had a particular interest in the idea of the unconscious.

You say, 'Yes, but why do you ask? I have heard of the unconscious. An analytic psychotherapist works with the unconscious.'

'When I read about psychotherapy, it mentioned that, but I have no idea what it is. It gave no explanation.'

'Where did you read about all this?'

'Wikipedia … and on the net. I was interested.'

'Good start, but the idea is controversial, not to say problematic. It can't be proved and if it's a part of the brain, it's not known where it is. We only know of its existence because of how it affects the everyday. Its roots lie in the emotional and the creative. Poets use their unconscious to see connections between things that are apparently not similar, as do artists, writers, and scientists. But it can work both ways, it can result in negative and destructive thoughts and behaviours.'

'I still don't get it.'

Okay, you say, 'Take that picture on the wall.' You point to the one of the woman wearing a parrot on her head. 'I don't know what it means. But the parrot has some meaning, otherwise why paint it? The artist might have dreamt this, but what of the woman in the picture? Maybe she feels okay with the parrot on her head, but why is it on her head? We just don't know the story.'

'But why should that interest you?'

'You sound amazed, but it's because it's symbolic of something. But what? … It's not obvious, is it? And here's another example. A woman arranges her collection of miniature gun turrets, cannons, and weapons on a table near her front door. They're all pointing towards whoever enters her house. Would you find that odd … assuming you noticed?'

He's silent at first, then he says, 'I guess it is odd.'

'It certainly is. Have you heard of Freud?

'Freud? Yes, who hasn't?'

Well, he worked with the patient's use of symbols and metaphors which he understood as representing the unconscious, but he also knew, for example, that sometimes a cigar is just a cigar.'

Silence, then he says, 'What's that mean?'

'It means what it says … a cigar is a cigar and nothing else … it has no other meaning.'

You take a quick look at him. He's looking straight ahead. 'I'm sorry I must have bored you but my work fascinates me.'

He turns to look at me with those penetrating eyes. You notice they're a deep blue and he has a small scar above one eyebrow. You wonder what's going on in his head. You think he's holding back on something, but you say nothing of your thoughts, 'The thing is the unconscious uses symbols and metaphors. That's its language.'

'You haven't bored me. On the contrary … but I must go.'

Again you say nothing. For a split second your eyes meet. You feel a little disappointment and it crosses your mind that maybe he was in two minds, that he didn't after all, really want to leave and that perhaps he'd like you to persuade him to stay.

'So,' you say 'why must you go?'

He stands up. 'I'm an only child. My father died in a car crash, my mother is permanently disabled. She's in a wheelchair and I'm the only carer.'

There was a hint of anger tinged with despair in this comment and the intensity and power in this revelation disconcerts you for a brief moment. So here was one clue to his depression, but you feel that's just the beginning.

'You live with her?'

'Yes.'

'And you have sole responsibility?' He nods, looks away from my gaze. I say, 'I'm really sorry.'

'Yes, it's bad. But I must go.'

He walks towards the door and is about to leave the room, when he stops, turns and says without looking at you, 'I feel like … shit … nearly all the time … sorry about that, my language, still he's not here, is he?'

You wonder if this is a reference to his dead father but make no comment. He continues, 'I'll think about what you've said … It's interesting. Maybe … but then … what's the point?' He didn't finish what he was saying, shrugged, shook his head, and walked out.

You guess you wouldn't ever see him again. You sit for a moment. You feel an overwhelming sense of sadness. You stand up and to distract yourself look at the picture of the woman with the parrot on her head. An inconsequential thought crosses your mind, one that amuses you. Could she really be as bird-brained as she looked? What did that say of the artist's relationship with the woman? … You leave and push your way through the partygoers, and without saying goodbye, you open the front door and run down the steps into the cool night air. You're conscious of feeling trapped and of the need to get out.

Later, talking with Emily, you find out his name is Harry, and that he's friendly with Toby, her husband. Silence. Toby had worked with him when they were both working on some computer networking issue. Initially Toby thought of him as quite aloof, but as he'd got to know him, although he'd said he'd lived alone, he'd picked up there was more to it than that. But Harry had never confided in him.

Emily says, 'I told Toby he's probably autistic.'

'Why do you say that?

'Because Toby said he never says anything about himself, or shows emotion, or humour. He said he's difficult.'

'Maybe he's depressed,' you say, 'isn't that possible?'

'Well, if he is, he should go to the doctor and not make other people feel bad'.

'Actually Emily, I'd never thought you were like that.'

'Like what?'

'What you've just said. You're like a member of the "pull up your socks" brigade … and you've labelled him … with a diagnosis. You've made some kind of judgement about him and it's not a good look.'

She was embarrassed, 'Sorry' she said, 'But you would think like that. You're a therapist. I don't want to fall out with you. But he's strange.'

You sigh, 'Strange? Maybe, a better and more accurate description would be "estranged". She looks blankly at you. 'Think about it', you say.

Personal

'Suffering comes in many forms and many shades, and the ability to recognise and communicate these lay the foundations for becoming a psychotherapist. Furthermore, in relationship to the experience of an injustice or a trauma, when advised to 'forget it' or 'put it behind you' it doesn't work. In fact, I came to understand that this attitude is powerfully and personally political, because it is linked to repression. The person who turns away from a trauma, an abuse, a mad-making relationship, a disturbing account, leaves the other isolated and alone. Silence is not an option or a solution. To speak out is a necessary step in understanding, and comes before its acceptance, and before the tentative, slow flowering of resilience, as in the following personal account.'

— CHAPTER 4 —

Beginnings

Rarely am I asked in a straightforward way why I became a psychotherapist. A more usual response is a silence followed by, 'I could never be a therapist', then, 'How can you tolerate listening to people's problems day after day?', or 'Are you analysing me?' I've only occasionally responded, primarily because for years I didn't know myself, but now I do, even though only partially. So I have an answer to the question, which you may be wondering; why choose to be a psychotherapist?

But 'choose' is probably too strong a word. I might have chosen to sell handmade birthday cards, or become a dentist, an engineer, an interior designer, even though the latter, with its focus on rearranging internal spaces, thinking metaphorically, does have certain similarities with psychotherapy. But even so, I didn't choose any of these. The motives for becoming any particular occupation will vary but there are always the elements of drift and luck. Either or both, may present particular opportunities and my life was no different.

I became a therapist because it felt the right thing to do. I was drawn to the work because it was easy for me to imagine, and in some instances identify with how troubled, how angry, and isolated, someone might really feel. After all, I had a reservoir of my own experiences to draw on, but eventually I also discovered I could put into words how I felt, and correspondingly how others might feel, so there was a kind of inbuilt connection between myself and others. It was and is, 'a transferable skill'.

Many decades ago, Carl Jung, a contemporary and colleague of Freud was one of the first to observe and comment on the childhood background of many therapists. Often they had had a trauma of their own, and these experiences were fundamental to his notion of, 'the wounded healer.' Certain experiences in childhood made it more likely they could identify with a patient's stress and hurt, and also more likely to be empathic and sensitive. This is not a rule but a tendency, since within the general population there are likely to be empathic individuals who are not healers, or alternatively potential healers who despite a background of trauma fail to identify or understand another's pain.

However, at the same time, Jung urged caution. In some instances, such was the power of the patient's transference and the therapist's countertransference,[8] the patient's need to be heard and understood were lost in the therapist's own history. In such cases, Jung stressed the necessity for the therapist to receive further and extensive individual psychotherapy of their own.

Throughout my own therapy, I became increasingly aware of the importance of Jung's observations on the impact of trauma. A childhood trauma attacks and undermines trust in the adult world, along with the expectation of predictability and security, but I survived by standing back, observing, and making sense of what

---

8   A reference to a fundamental technique within analytic psychotherapy which enables the therapist to understand the patient's communication. The transference is the communication via words and feeling of a patient's earlier experience. The countertransference is the therapist's emotional response to the patient's communication but articulated in such a way, it enables the patient to make connections with their past and their present troubles. For some examples of this process, See the conversation in Part One when the therapist becomes aware of her own feelings as she listens to Harry, although her countertransference remains uncommunicated.

I heard. This also included, because of certain experiences and my response to them, a wariness about particular people together with a sensitivity towards what might be called, an underlying callousness, a cruelty glossed over by its entertainment value. For example, when some event is dressed up as amusing, as a medical procedure, or as 'a dark art', all may be passed off as insignificant. Life and people are not always what they seem and I knew this from an early age.

We all find different ways to survive, and how we make sense of our life is part of that. To psychically take hold of life with its myriad experiences, doubts, confusions, truths and hopes, necessarily takes courage to break the silence. Because whether understood literally or metaphorically, a silence acts like a deadweight on the mind, crushing creativity and censoring spontaneity.

— CHAPTER 5 —

A Childhood

My mother, age nineteen, worked in central Birmingham in a dress shop. My father had been cast out into the wilderness by my mother for reasons unknown to me, and I was placed in the daily care of my mother's aunt and uncle. All three rowed and this could be initiated by any one of them. Afterwards my mother would drag me back to her father's house, but it was always temporary, because eventually and inevitably, we'd return. Until the next time.

    I remember those rows. The dark images of anger are held like a sudden snapshot in my mind. I remember the times I'd creep away and block my ears from the yelling and silently sidle up the dark staircase and hide in the empty bedroom at the top of the house and crouch on the floor and through the window I'd watch the buses stop and the passengers stream off and walk home. The rows occurred without warning, they just happened. It felt as if I'd been caught up in one of those pinball machines I'd seen in my grandfather's club, and just like pinballs, we, my mother and I, bounced and ricocheted, mindlessly and erratically, between one part of Birmingham to another.

I was about five when my mother told me we were going to permanently move back to her father's house. This was about three miles away. She said she was sick of the constant rows. She said the rows were my aunt's fault. She said that my aunt had told her she didn't look after me properly and that she stopped me from seeing my father. She said it was none of her business and she'd be glad to go, and that it was about time anyway, because I'd be starting school soon. She said she no longer needed my aunt and uncle to look after me.

I listened but I said nothing. I was young, but even at that age, I knew how to keep my mouth shut, because saying the wrong thing or at the wrong time to any of them could cause a row to break out. But secretly I thought and hoped, that if we did move, a change of scenery and people might mean the rows would stop. It didn't happen.

My mother lived, it seemed, in a perpetual state of irritation which meant within minutes, she'd work herself up into full blown anger. As soon as the day broke and she lifted her head from the pillow, she'd start. She had the eyes of a night hawk and a tongue like a whiplash. Cruel but funny, you didn't want to get on the wrong side of her. 'Look at her legs, just like a piece of knotted string'. 'A face only a mother could love.' 'If she thinks her hair looks good, she's wrong. It's like a yard of pump water.' 'Mutton dressed as lamb.' 'She'd do better to keep her mouth shut.'

The only things that cheered her up were clothes. She worked in a dress shop and she'd occasionally bring home a dress and try it on, posing and smiling in front of the mirror at her image. Before long I found out the best way to put her in a good mood. I'd tell her how pretty she was, which was true, but if I really wanted to fast track her bad tempered snarls into simpering docility, I'd say something like, 'You know that man we see sometimes at the bus stop, he said to me that you had the looks of a film star.' That stopped her in her tracks. 'Really', she said, 'did he really say that?'

So we moved. For a time, we lived with her father, (my grandfather whom she hated), her stepmother, called Vera, (whom she ignored) and Vera's daughter, aged about eleven, (ditto, but additionally seen by all as an overweight nonentity). She went by the name of Jasmine. I rarely think of Jasmine but when I do, I think of her name. The absurdity of her name. How ridiculous it was. She was named after a Jasmine, the flower. How come that was her name? She had none of that flower's qualities. She lacked sweetness, delicacy or prettiness. If you think of their opposite, you'd be close to the mark. She'd have been better named, 'Deadly Nightshade.' She was a bully and practiced the skills of aggression and deviousness to a fine art.

When we left my aunt and uncle, they gave me a brand new blue bike. I loved that bike, its shininess, its colour, its small neatness, but as soon as Jasmine saw it, she offered to teach me to ride it. It was an offer I couldn't refuse. Try saying no to a bully. She had two favourite techniques. She'd either push me so fast, I'd fall off, or alternatively I'd start off slowly and wobble off at a reasonable pace, while she, running behind with one hand on the saddle, would suddenly jerk the bike when I was least expecting it, and I'd find myself pitched into the nettles and the long grass. She thought it was funny. I didn't and close to tears, I'd run off and lock myself in the toilet. I never told anyone. There would be no point.

The role of my mother from the start and throughout my childhood was always peripheral. She was like a 'stand in' or an understudy for the role of an idealised mother, while I waited off stage for the big moment when she appeared and dazzled the assembled audience with her beauty and wit. My role in her theatre and my childhood was to become her sidekick. I became adept in gauging the right time and finding the right words to feed her the right lines. She had a Chaucerian personality, and like the Wife of Bath, she was the biggest flirt that ever set foot on this planet.

By way of contrast, she liked poetry, especially the poetry of Dylan Thomas, and she had the potential to be a sculptor. She could take a piece of clay and as I watched, she'd mould it between her fingers until a human face would gradually appear. At her best she could be funny, assuming you could cope with the possible 'put downs' which were a daily occurrence.

She was also a good conversationalist, but being maternal was a quality unknown to her. Throughout the whole of my childhood, I have no memory of a kind or loving word or action from her or her husband, my step father, towards me, ever. The Americans have coined a phrase for such behaviour. They call them 'micro-aggressions'; these are the daily thoughtless, verbal or non-verbal scimitars which cut through to a child's soul. I still bear those psychic marks, although mostly they remain hidden. This was not the case with my great aunt and uncle, her aunt and uncle. They made up for her harsh outlook on life, and consequently I have loving memories of both of them. They gave me what she was incapable of giving.

It was in this part of my life, while we were living with the people above, the road accident occurred. Everyone knows the expression, 'Accidents happen' and no one argues against it. Like the 'Act of God' clause in an insurance policy, it is presented as an incontrovertible truth. No one is to blame, and we live to see another day, or most of us do. But the reality is, accidents, especially traumatising accidents which are classified as 'life changing' have both causes and effects. These may be physical or emotional, but both can be crippling, albeit in different ways. Yet such moments of 'force majeure' may offer the possibility of a positive development. In my case, I think the experience laid the foundations for my becoming a therapist.

— CHAPTER 6 —

The Accident

My mother asked Jasmine to meet me from school. But she forgot. She never came. I waited for her alone in the school playground. She was a few years older than me, so maybe my mother thought she was old enough to be responsible. That's all I know. Nobody ever talked about it, then or later. The event disappeared into the past for them, but not for me. It remains in my memory to this day.

Jasmine forgot.

What does that feel like? I was five, nearly six. I waited. I waited. You want to know for how long? Until I knew she'd forgotten. I was totally alone. I remember looking around. The playground empty. No teachers, no children shouting, pushing, jumping, laughing. Just me. And my bike. The silence of an empty playground.

I look at my bike. It's lying on the floor. I pick it up. I want to go home, I want to see my aunt and uncle. I start pushing my bike along the pavement. I want to go back to them. I'm not sure of the way. I am about to cross the road.

It's a main road. I can see a lorry. I'm holding my bike. My hands are tight round the handlebars. The lorry. I'm halfway across the road. It's coming towards me. I'm staring at it. I'm holding my bike so tight. My fingers are white. I stand there. It's not stopping.

It's nearer, it gets nearer … Loud, so loud. The noise. Deafens. It's still coming, It doesn't stop. I'm staring at it. It's almost on me.

Silence.

I can't move. I can't move. I can't breathe.

The world has stopped.

Silence.

A man is leaning over me. He's talking. I don't understand what he's saying.

I'm on my back.

I'm being wheeled out into a building.

People in the street stop. They stare.

I'm in a corridor. It's too noisy. It's too bright. It's too crowded.

Nothing is real. Alone. I'm in hospital.

I'm lying on a trolley whimpering like a wounded animal. I'm drowning in the light. I'm assaulted by the noise. A man in a white coat approaches. He smiles. He leans over me. With his scissors he begins cutting away my clothes. I feel the hard, cold steel of the scissors against the heat of my skin. The pain is brutal. I cry out. I scream. I beg him to stop.

He says he has to do this. He continues, nothing stops him.

He says I was brave. Brave? How could I be brave, when I shed so many tears.

I remember nothing more. When I wake, my leg is suspended, attached to the ceiling via a pulley from the high iron frame surrounding the bed. I lie in a ward of children, injured, who faced with unimaginable suffering, have lapsed into a mute silence. I can see them. No one speaks.

I have only my thoughts to keep me company.

I think about the times when I played in the park. Nothing will ever be the same. Nothing can be the same.

Once I was free. Once I was happy, but now?

Immobile. Trapped. The bed is my home, the ward my world, the white wall my neighbour.

My mind flits back and forth. Day after day. Night follows night.

Time measured in dull routines.

Where are you when you have no clock, no watch, no calendar.

The night nurse, then the day nurse, one follows the other.

A monotonous exchange, a routine of nothingness, imprisoned in a bed, somewhere unknown, somewhere alone.

Time passes.

People in white coats, hushed, serious, stand, whisper at the end of my bed.

They move on. Why don't you talk to me? I'm here.

In my bed, watching, waiting, listening.

Do they know who I am? Does anyone care?

I remember the yellow glow of the hospital nights. The sound of a child crying. Long, pathetic wails, sudden sobs, choking and filling the air. Then the silence. The silence. The silence.

The nurse sits by the child's bed. She is talking to her. She is quiet now. What does she say? Does she say it's alright, and do you believe her?

I cannot cry. I feel nothing. This is how it is. Day after day and night after night. Waiting, waiting, waiting. I hide, hide under the cloak of my indifference. Isolation crushes my spirit.

Today I turn my head to look at the boy in the next bed. Like me, his leg is suspended in the iron cradle. He tells me if I stand on my one good leg and twist around, I can see through the window. I do what he says. The sky is grey. I look down. The people are small and insignificant. They hurry to work. They're far away. In another world. They know nothing of the life I live now. The boy jumps up and down on his one leg until the whole bed rocks.

Suddenly I laugh. He has made me laugh.

A nurse tells him to stop.

I remember the meal times. The little table set for little people. A table laid, all neat and nice where little children eat. I think of the book my aunt had given me. On the cover, Snow White and the Seven Dwarfs. Just like now. But not quite. That was before, and that was a story. This is now. This is real. Is the book still where I left it? Do you remember me? I'm here now, and there is no Snow White. Do you know that?

I'm thinking now about the green bus, the green double decker bus that used to stop outside my great aunt and uncle's shop. I'd look at the passengers sitting inside and I'd wonder why their faces look as if they were pasted onto the inside of the window. Once, after the bus had rumbled away, one of the passengers came into the shop, and asked who I was.

'She's my niece's child, we're looking after her while her mother works. Her name's Marguerite. 'She's certainly a bonny girl.'

I'd feel myself screw up inside with embarrassment and I'd remove myself into the kitchen away from prying eyes, and I'd wonder what 'bonny' meant, but I never asked. I loved my aunt and uncle and even after all these years I have good memories of them.

I remember the time when my uncle took me to a circus. I wanted to be a tightrope walker. I insisted he stretched a piece of rope in the back garden from one point to another, so I could be like her, a tightrope walker. But the inevitable happened. Even as he held my hand, the rope sagged and I found it impossible to balance on the rope even with his help.

He'd let me find out for myself one of life's lessons, that sometimes, no matter how much we want something, it just doesn't work out.

My aunt bought me books with stories and pictures of colourful animals who lived in the forest. A hedgehog with a pink, pointed nose, and Bambi whose eyes were always filled with tears. Out of them all, I loved Bambi the best. I believed they talked, laughed, cried, and lived as families in the rustic kitchens and bedrooms built inside the massive, gnarled roots of the woodland trees. My aunt would chat to me about the customers coming into the shop as if we were the same age and close gossipy friends, and she'd tell me what her views were and ask if I'd noticed certain individuals, and then she'd say what she thought about them. I miss her.

She was the only one who ever mentioned my father. I don't remember ever seeing him, but she told me what a decent man he was and that she couldn't understand why my mother had left him. I can't remember him ever coming to hospital to see me, or my mother, or anybody for that matter. As for my mother, I had no memories of her at all during those early days.

I remember the day a girl got off the bus. It stopped outside where we lived. She looked about the same age as me and she was holding her mother's hand. I ran down the stairs and watched them walk down the road until they turned into a house opposite the park. I wanted to be friends, so I hang around their house until the girl noticed me. She has a small pram and I ask if my doll could have a ride in her pram with her doll. Soon we met every day. My friend's mother agreed to keep an eye on us, so we were free to play in her house. We take our dolls for regular outings to the park and we play on the swings to see who can swing the highest. I was happy then.

I am being wheeled along a long corridor on a trolley to a white room. My mother's there, together with lots of doctors. I hate it. They're dressed in starched, white clinical coats. Some of them have pens inserted in their top pockets. She's dressed in her favourite ocelot coat. That's what she called it. It's like the skin of a jungle animal and I don't like it. However, It seems to make her happy because she's smiling all the time. There's the usual smell of disinfectant in the room. One of the doctors says hello to me. I don't reply.. I want to run away, but I can't. It's as if I'm not there, as if I'm invisible.

They hold up X-rays against the light. They ask me to walk back and forth across the room. They look at the X-rays and how I walk.

They measure my legs. They consider whether one leg is shorter. I listen, and one of them says, for a compound fracture of the femur, it's healed well. They say to my mother that I can leave the hospital but I must do exercises.

She looks at them and then she laughs—a tinkling laugh. I watch her. I watch them all. The doctor is laughing. She's laughing. I don't know why they're laughing. But I do now. I understand. She was flirting. She's a flirt. She's a mother. She's my mother and she's young and pretty, but I feel no affection for her, only curiosity. I don't know her and she doesn't know me.

— CHAPTER 7 —

Lost in Time and Space

Here I am, it's the same place with the same people, but I'm different. I'm older, much older. The image of the lorry is still there. It's in my head. I've survived. But not quite. I don't feel real. My uncle says I have an old head on young shoulders but when I ask what he means, he just laughs. Time has lost any meaning for me. I'm disorientated. I might just as well be floating about in a gravity-less space capsule, endlessly circling the earth. I have no routine and no home.

I'm still the same child who tried to be a tightrope walker on the clothes line, the same child who took her dolls for walks in her friend's pram, and loved to swing in the park. The experience in the hospital has changed me. Death, injury and pain I know about, but what of betrayal? Yes, I know of that too.

Life continues. I miss my aunt and uncle. But I notice things. Like my mother says one thing, but does something else. I say nothing. Self-delusion is necessary for some to psychologically survive and I knew this from an early age. But I also knew that this talent, if that's what it is, necessarily has to go with keeping one's mouth shut.

Nobody likes being told, particularly by a child, they're contradicting themselves. I learnt that too.

Two weeks after leaving the hospital my mother says she is about to marry the man called Spike. Is this the man I first met in hospital.? She continues talking. I continue thinking. She doesn't notice. She has no expectation or interest whether I am listening or what I might say or think, so I remain silent. My mind is elsewhere.

I'm away and remembering something from the hospital. It's vivid. It's as if real. It's not a dream. I'm lying in a bed in a white room. It's an operating theatre. My mother enters with a man. If she introduced him or said who he was, I didn't take it in. I have other things on my mind. Like I am about to die. That's what I was thinking.

He was irrelevant, an intrusive stranger. How pleased with himself he looks. He's grinning like a Cheshire Cat, so much so I feel like punching him in the face. I want him out. A nurse fits a mask on my face and nose, and as I breathe in, the room dissolves from its totality of whiteness into an absence. An absence. A nothingness. I have no consciousness. I've gone. Nothing matters anymore. I've left the world.

My mother continues to talk. She's oblivious to me. She knows nothing of me or of my thoughts. Her talk pulls me back into the present. She's telling me again that she's about to marry him. I'm thinking as she speaks that while I was in hospital, she was busy meeting other men. I'm aware of a flash of anger. It lasts a microsecond. Nice one. Did she discard the first one, my father, before she started her search for the second? Where is he anyway?

She doesn't say and I don't ask because actually, I don't care. I'm immune. I feel indifferent to anything she says or does. She asks if I'd like to choose a new dress for the wedding. 'Yes, I'd like a red one.' She chooses a brown and white one. It's made of organdie and is pretty but it's not red. Why ask, I think, if you have no intention of taking any notice of what the other person says. Then she tells me, we're going to move to Cardiff from Birmingham to live in her future husband's parents' house.

From the intensity and the slow drama of the hospital, It's now life in the fast lane. The speed of decision making is impressive and I'm forced, whether I like it or not, to be dragged along in their slip stream. Within two weeks of leaving hospital, I've left my aunt and my uncle, moved to a new city, lost a father, gained a stepfather, and moved in with his parents. Good or bad? I was about to find out but knowing life as I did, things could get a whole lot worse. I was right on that score.

My mother and Spike marry and I discover that memory is a strange thing. I've managed to obliterate all experiences of the wedding, with the one exception. By mistake, I tear the organdie dress. My mother is not pleased. I remember that. She has a temper and she frightens me with her anger. Years later and I'm looking at a photo of the wedding. It's in black and white and I'm standing at the front. I have a white bow in my hair. I have no idea of the people grouped behind me. Who are they? I'm twisting my hands. I look uncertain and nervous. Her new husband's hands are on my shoulders; probably to stop me running away, which is what I'd like to do.

After the wedding, my mother's new husband, the man who became my stepfather speaks to me. This might be a day after the wedding, or a week after, or a year after. Time had lost its meaning.. But I remember this. We're in the house in Cardiff. We're standing at the bottom of the stairs.

He's caught me on my own. I'm cornered. There's no escape. He says to me I must call him dad. These are words without meaning. He has a certain manner about him, self-satisfied, cold, his facial expression determined, his eyes pale blue and hard, his mouth a tight straight line. I don't like him. I look at him. I'm thinking how ugly he is.

Doesn't he know I already have a dad? He lives in Birmingham. What's happened to him? But I didn't say a word. The idea of calling him dad chokes me. I feel suffocated with the word. For years, I avoid using the word. Sometimes it's difficult. Sometimes I have to use it, but every time I do, I feel the lie. He is not my father and I don't like to lie for him. Every time I'm forced to use that name, I feel I've betrayed myself. What was he talking about? I have no idea. I say nothing. Not one word. There was no point. No one would have listened. Beside they were the liars. Before living there, I hadn't known grown-ups lie. Now I knew. They could and they did.

And here's something else that happened. It's burnt into my soul. I'm attending a new school. I overhear a conversation that I'm going to be put in a low stream, a B stream, because I'd missed so much school. When I started this school I had one surname but within two weeks I have another, and this new surname replaces the original.

I'm given a note by my mother and I'm told to give it to the teacher. I did as I was told.

I'm standing at the front of the class by her desk. She silently reads it and then she turns to me and says, 'Do you know what's in this note, Marguerite?' I reply that I don't.

'Well, it says from now on, we're to call you, Marguerite Hughes.'

I say, 'But my name is Jones.'

She replies, 'Not any more, it isn't.'

I feel a cold rage. Rebellion touches my soul. How dare they. A new identity signed, sealed, and delivered. My past systematically destroyed. Who am I? I no longer knew. No one mentions my aunt and my uncle or my father. Gradually a mood comes over me. Living in that house in Cardiff fills me with an anger and a strange, crushing boredom. I withdraw into myself.

The claustrophobia and noise of the hospital is now replaced with the dark walls and low ceilings of that house and the stupidity and conventionality of the people who lived there. It was there I learnt, without complaint, to silently endure hopelessness and despair.

Disapproval and resentment was on the menu and like meat and drink, it was served daily. They loved that diet, even though it gave them indigestion. Maybe they loved that too. They resent my presence. They know nothing about me but worse, I'm condemned to silence.

* * *

I am displaced, a child with no past whose name has been changed. The days were the worst. They stare at me. They talk about me behind my back. I am the daughter of a divorced woman and I'd been in hospital for weeks, but the hospital was never referred to, and nobody asked me about it. No one speaks, no one. The hospital. The accident. Airbrushed out of existence, I'm on my own. With an anger that cannot be voiced. I was an alien in a world of smug, profoundly stupid adults.

Silenced. Gagged, I didn't fit in. She looks like a gypsy I hear one of them say. Intended as an insult, I turn it into a compliment. I felt like a gypsy. I wanted to be wild like a gypsy. I'd seen things, heard things, they knew nothing of and never would, but worse, they didn't want to know. So I was left with it. The drip, drip of the emotional poison, the fear, the confusion, the sense of betrayal that came with the lonely jolt of a sudden memory. Nothing can stop that.

Was I wild? A child of nature? Was I angry? Of course I was angry. For three months I'd survived life in a virtual war zone. I'd lived on a ward with children screaming with unimaginable pain and loss, permanently scarred by all that life had unfairly thrown at them. That's what I would have said at the time … if I'd been asked, but nobody asked because nobody wanted to know.

Why was thar? Guilt? Indifference? Lack of imagination? I existed in an environment of suffocatingly respectability and blandness. War and peace. I'd lived in both. Real or virtual? Which was worse? The actual or the imagined? Did anyone care? I think not. For them, it was 'put up or shut up'. Feelings were seen as a sign of madness. I learnt to keep silent.

As I write this account of my thoughts and feelings of the post hospital experiences, it came to mind that gradually and unexpectedly, there were times when, to use the words of one of Dylan Thomas' poem 'Light breaks where no sun shines.'[9]

---

9 Dylan Thomas, 'Light breaks where no sun shines', 1937. https://poets.org/poem/light-breaks-where-no-sun-shines

The music of jazz. Jazz is the music of the dispossessed and of the soul. It's the music of loss and yearning. It spoke to me then and still does. My mother's brother-in-law was a jazz drummer and he lived in the same house. Recently in his memory and of my six year old self, I wrote the following which I now dedicate to all jazz drummers. It's a metaphoric appreciation 'of a personal history and the passage of time.

Jazz drummers play with Time

A jazz drummer, my mother's brother-in-law,
plays the drums,
smiles a smile behind his glasses,
then bends, slides, brushes the skin of the drum between his knees,
and now
a pause,
a quiet,
a stillness,
that waits
to be broken.
by the beat and the heat and the passage of time.
Play with it, catch it, hold it, let it go, let it fly,
do it right. Time it right,
play it ahead. Play it behind.
Follow the rhythm of the beat
Because jazz drummers play with time
I hold my breath and I wait
for the rhythm, the heat of the beat, in the silence of time.

I begin roaming the back streets. Gradually I stop going to school. No one notices. It's a bid for freedom It was a while before they found out but it was just long enough to find myself. I'd had enough. Their indifference was all encompassing, I felt suffocated. I'd been told how to get to school. One day, I didn't go. I went to the park just down the road. It had a large boating lake and I sat on the grass for a while watching people row. A boy, a little older, came over to speak to me. He asked who I was. I said I was new and I used to live in Birmingham and I didn't want to go school. He asked whether I'd like to come with him and climb trees. I said yes. Like me, he was a truant. On the run, an early compatriot, a comrade in arms. Those were happy days.

He knew, he understood. Words were not necessary. He lived in a neighbouring house with a monkey puzzle tree in the garden. I didn't like the tree but I liked him. He was eleven, a few years older than me, but we were friends.

For two weeks we ran wild. We didn't bother with school. We behaved as if we'd been granted the freedom of the City of Cardiff. We rode on the buses, the front top seats with the best view (free) we played in the park and found secret places where we hid (free) and we climbed trees and looked down on people passing below (free) and we played on the railway lines and balanced our way round the huge water tanks for the trains. We knew no danger.

We spun and wheeled with the freedom of swallows flying through the wide summer sky. We did what we liked, where we liked, and when we liked. Free of lies, stupidity, meaningless rules, manipulation, coercion, convention, and disapproval, those times were wonderful. I was happy. But it couldn't and didn't last. Now I have no memory of his name or what he looked like.

After we were discovered, he disappeared from my life, but I remember the times with him. I remember how I felt. I remember the excitement. I remember the freedom. I remember the sun shone. I remember my joy. He gave me my first therapeutic experience; acceptance and understanding. For all I know he was a member of a problem family. For all I know he was destined to become a delinquent, but he gave me back that sense of who I was, and he liked me. So even though I never saw him again, and I have forgotten his name, I shall never forget him. He lives on in my mind.

After I'd been caught truanting, I was given a series of tests, presumably with an educational psychologist, and unsurprisingly, I was way behind in my school work. I received extra lessons and within weeks I was promoted to an A stream. One of those teachers gave me the greatest gift of all, she taught me to read, and it was this love of books which subsequently carried me through the troubles of childhood.

Books. Throughout those times, I read constantly and obsessively. I lived my life through books. As I finished one book, another would be ready and waiting for me. Libraries were my friend. I could escape into another world. While I read, I could lose myself and ignore the people around me. I lived in my own world, I was somewhere else. A private world of my own making. A place where I was safe. A place where I could hide.

The lives of a book's characters totally enthralled me and by the time I reached my mid-teens, I was totally engaged with the richness of the narratives, the description of the places, and the characters of Victorian novels. I was enthralled with the observations of Thomas Hardy and his tales of unfulfilled longing and life's injustices, with George Eliot for her psychological and philosophical insights, and with the Brontës' for their preoccupation with the wild landscapes and characters of West Yorkshire. The translations of Flaubert, Balzac and Zola were also similarly gripping, but one story in particular stayed with me over all the years, and it was not a classic, but more of a horror story. I remember it, because it contained a powerful metaphor for my underlying depression.

    I was still a child but I had borrowed the book from the adult section. The story revolved around an empty black sack that apparently lay lifeless in a room. During the hours of darkness, it came randomly alive and enveloped and smothered anybody in its path. This possibility haunted my imagination. Many years later having started my own psychotherapy I understood its meaning. It was the fear of my own dormant depression symbolised by the suffocating of life by the black sack.

Childhood for me, was a matter of survival. Apart from my love of reading, it was difficult. As previously noted, my mother's gifts were not maternal and by my early to mid-teens I really came to see this for what it was. People knew of my mother. Known as a big personality, she had to be the centre of attention. She could be cringingly embarrassing, like the time at her own party, she mimicked being a stripper to a piece of music with the same name. This was her public persona, but there was another side to her.

As I entered my teens, her overly critical attitudes towards me increased. She watched me like a cat poised for the kill. To the list of things already wrong with me, she now added her disapproval of how I looked and behaved—like a tart apparently. Half the time, I had no idea what she was talking about although I observed her interest in my real or imagined relationship with boys and my stepfather's interest in my body. Once I came home early to find him rifling through my drawers and reading my diary. His comments were often inappropriate and intrusive but I learned to feign deafness and ignore them.

I disliked my stepfather. He was not my father. Throughout my whole childhood I was always aware of the lies they told. I secretly and strongly objected to him being introduced to neighbours and their friends as my father, and of the unspoken veto on ever referring to my own father. Maybe he was aware of my simmering hostility towards him. Maybe he saw in me, a wild anarchic spirit which offended his suburban predictability. But whatever the cause, he developed a refined and subtle response to put me in my place. It was a masterclass in hostility. He behaved as if I didn't exist.

Simple but effective, days would go by without him addressing me or acknowledging my presence, although he occasionally reminded me in one way or another, that he was watching me. His speciality was the sneer. A sneer, simple, cheap, and legal, and barely noted as a form of child abuse, goes a long way in its capacity to emotionally hurt a child.

However, since they (neither parent) had made little or no attempt to keep in touch with my aunt and uncle or my father, and having no one else to turn to, I occasionally voiced my distress and unhappiness with him, to my mother.

Her response? 'You should be grateful he's taken you on. He didn't have to.'

The fact I had no choice or I might have feelings about the whole issue didn't occur to either of them and even if it had, it would have been treated with total indifference. It was some years later when we were living near Sandringham in Norfolk when I came to the decision to leave home. I remember attending a GP for depression on my own, which was usual. Most things I had learnt to do on my own. I was probably aged about fifteen or sixteen. I also remember at the same time, my mother was very impressed with the knowledge that I was to see the same doctor as the Queen. She showed less or no interest in my unhappiness. In fact, my low mood irritated them both and on more than one occasion, I overheard them complaining about me to their friends, including the local postman.

I'd been standing in my bedroom with the window open as I heard my mother regaling the postman with my many faults. Apart from my appearance and wearing too much lipstick, apparently, I didn't smile or laugh enough and 'I was a misery to be around.' After a few inconsequential questions, the doctor subsequently diagnosed 'endogenous depression' and that was it.

However, somehow and somewhere, I had come across the name and history of Sigmund Freud. I decided to look him up in the local Reference Library. His writing intrigued me but soon I discovered his work was too complex and way above my head for it to make much sense. But there was one exception, and that was his use of the term, 'insecurity'. This word carried all the feelings and thoughts I experienced. Of displacement, of not fitting in, of being different, of not being liked or loved, together with the deep anxiety that at any minute things could change catastrophically.

— CHAPTER 8 —

Rites of Passage—Rum and Blackcurrant

I was seventeen and I'd been staying with a friend by the name of Joanne, called Jo for short, and her mother was a friend of my mother. The four of us rather bizarrely had gone on holiday to Wales in a dormobile, driven by my mother who very recently had passed her driving test. The only memory I have of this holiday, was my mother's driving inexperience.

Manoeuvring the van round a hairpin bend on a hill in Pembrokeshire, we found ourselves alarmingly gently rolling backwards. Fortunately we were rescued by an oncoming motorist who jumped out of his car and shouted to her to pull on the handbrake. The van having come to a stop, he then took over the controls and drove the van safely to an off-road stopping area. After this trip, she had driven back to Norfolk to return the vehicle, leaving me on a temporary basis with Jo and her family, who lived in Kent.

It was my first taste of freedom. I discovered my friend's mother was very different to my own and that she seemed interested and supportive of both of us. Or that's how it seemed. 'Seemed' is just about the right word. Neither Jo or myself had any educational qualifications and we were in no rush to work, especially as I had no idea of what I should do. But that didn't seem to matter. Jo had an elder brother called Ben who rode a motorbike and right from the start there was the zing of a strong attraction.

These feelings were new to me. I liked his quietness, his thoughtful hazel eyes, his smile, and his tanned complexion, his floppy brown straight hair. But neither of us said anything and this mutual attraction, was as far as I knew, an unspoken secret between the two us.

One Saturday Jo went shopping with her mother, leaving Ben and I alone. He suggested we go for a ride on his motorbike. I can't say I was enthusiastic but I went, albeit somewhat reluctantly. It was a short ride. He could tell I wasn't too impressed. Actually I was scared he might crash, and I'd fall off.

On our return, he asked me if I'd like a drink. He suggested rum and blackcurrant. The blackcurrant was in a kitchen cupboard and the rum was kept in a glass cabinet in their dining room. It was mid-afternoon. It was an interesting offer.

I considered it, before saying, 'I don't think so, I've never had alcohol before.' To be truthful, I had had a small amount of alcohol before, but not 'rum and black' and not alone with a man I saw as attractive.

He persisted and said, 'Try some ... see if you like it.' I gave him a look. I wasn't quite sure what was going on, but he ignored my suspicions. He poured out the rum, then the blackcurrant, and handed me the glass. I took a sip. It had a strong, warm, fruity taste. I held the drink up to the light and admiring its deep purple colour, I drank more.

'Yes, I like it' I said. 'It's sweet'

I finished the glass and after a moment's hesitation, I again put forward my glass.

He filled it to the brim and then said helpfully, 'Drink it slowly. You're not meant to drink so fast.'

My mood changed. A woman on a mission, I decided I was going to get drunk. I liked the careless feeling and the ensuing warm glow that came with the effects of alcohol, and for the moment I wanted to share this feeling with him. I said, 'It's like Ribena with a kick in it, but why aren't you having more?' I had noticed that despite what he said, he was having far less than me.

'Of course I will. More?'

I put my glass out again. Ben poured another. It was larger than the first, but I didn't object. We stood opposite each other. Neither of us spoke. Ben sat down on the sofa and smiling, patted the seat beside him. We sat awkwardly side by side. There was a long silence.

'Have another one.'

I ignored the gradual signs of the dizziness, I felt. The truth was I was enjoying the freedom that came with feeling light headed. I leant back and gazed round the room. Ben moved closer. I stayed put. I picked up a magazine and flicked through the pages. I glanced at him. A thought came and went. It was about how good looking he was. It took a while before I replied. Some warning thoughts had passed through my mind, that I should be careful because at any moment, Jo and her mother might return from shopping.

Rather reluctantly I said, 'I don't think I should.'

'Why not? I'll match you.'

'Because it's going to my head.'

'Isn't that good?'

I looked at him. I began wondering what his game was, but I wasn't an innocent. I'd read enough books to fill a second hand bookshop. I decided to speak out. It was time to back off.

'Have you read *Cider with Rosie*?'

'Nope. I don't read.'

'That's a shame.'

'I'm an engineer. I read manuals … about machines.'

'Not the same.'

'Probably not. I'm a practical man.'

'The book's about seduction … at least some of it is … it's about a boy and a girl who live in the country, in the Cotswolds, to be precise and one hot afternoon they get together to drink cider, lots of it, and then ... why are you smiling?'

'No reason'.

'Well, it's not funny.'

'What isn't?'

'Seduction'.

'No, it's not funny at all ... rather nice, I'd say.'

He glanced away and then turned his head to look straight at me. It was a full on eye contact. I was out of my depth. I sighed and avoiding his eyes looked across the room.

An awkward conversation stuttered into existence. Totally meaningless fragments of sentences, whereby neither of us knew what to say or when to say whatever tangled thoughts lay inside our heads. There was a long silence ... again.

I said, 'I have to admit, I don't know what to say.'

'You don't have to say anything.'

I took another sip, ignoring the fact I was feeling more than queasy.

Quite suddenly, I stood up and I said, 'I'm going to the bathroom. I'm going to be sick.'

'I did say, don't drink so fast.'

'I don't feel well ... I need to go to the loo.'

He stood up. 'Let me take you.'

'I know where to go. I live here, don't forget ... or at least I do ... for the time being ...'

'Stop talking. I want to look after you.'

I gave him a look and then I laughed, 'That'll be a first. Look after me ...' I had a good line in sarcasm. Learnt probably from my mother.

'What's so funny? You need looking after ... I thought that when I first saw you.'

'Really ... so ... what are you going to do? My tone was challenging.

'If you're not well.' He took my hand. 'You need to go bed'

I removed my hand. 'I'm going to be sick ...'

'I'm sorry.'

'You should be.'

I abruptly left the room and slowly and carefully made my way up the stairs. Ben followed. I paused at the door of my bedroom. He walked in, sat on my bed and said, 'I'll wait for you here.'

I lurched into the bathroom, locked the door, and threw up. I studied my face in the mirror. I was deadly pale and having trouble standing. I was there for some time, waiting for the waves of sickness to subside. I left the bathroom. My bedroom door was shut and when I opened it, I could see Ben was asleep and he lay, fully clothed, on my bed. I shut the bedroom door. By now, I couldn't care less about anything. I flung myself down beside him, and immediately fell asleep.

It was almost dark when I woke up. I sat up. I could hear Jo, her mother and her father talking downstairs. I glanced at Ben. He was awake and lying on his back contemplating the ceiling. Neither of us spoke. He sat up, took my hand and said, 'We'd better get up … they're back'. I didn't reply. He left the bedroom. I followed five minutes later by myself.

We were met with a wall of silent disapproval. The silence continued for several days. I was consumed with guilt and embarrassment. Even Jo avoided talking to me. All conversation was cursory and since Ben went to work during the day, I felt abandoned and like a pariah in their house. I had no idea what to do or what to say. This dilemma didn't last long. It was resolved fairly quickly.

A week later, Jo's mother made an announcement. She had spoken with my mother. It had been agreed, she said formally, that a room in London would be found for me. She had found one in a Woman's Hostel somewhere in South West London, and she said, she would take me there. She had also arranged enough money to tide me over until I found work or put in a claim to Social Security.

How kind, how generous, I thought, more than a little ironically. I was seventeen. It felt very much like a rejection, a punishment for something. But what was it? Whatever they thought, was so shocking, so unsettling, and under their own roof, I, was to be evicted for something that hadn't happened. Whatever they imagined had to be stopped and the guilty, cast away. But I said nothing of this and as usual, I kept my mouth shut. I never saw Ben again. I never drank rum and blackcurrant again. I couldn't stand the sight or the smell of it. But I'd left home and I put a good spin on that. The excitement of London lay on the horizon. A new life was about to begin.

AND POLITICAL

'In the spring, the garden had a certain ambience about it. An otherworldliness of grace and elegance and even though an urban garden, it seemed to belong to another era, another place. The lawn was surrounded by a hedge of sweet smelling orange blossom, tall verbena, and the deep purple flower of the lilac. The flowers were carelessly abundant, their colours defiantly white and purple against the drab buildings in the background and seeing them filled me with joy. Their growth was magical; their presence so close to the mayhem of London traffic the garden seemed like an oasis, representing calmness and predictability. Yet understanding its personal significance came later, and only after I had sat and talked for some months in his drab, understated room.'

— CHAPTER 9 —

Lessons in Disillusionment: London Social Work

Social work in London is a little like undertaking a crash course in social anthropology. Wherever practiced, the range of ethnicities and the obvious differences of class, education and income, requires of the social worker the ability to tune into a sheer number of accents, idioms, and life styles. For example, the colourful, picturesque and often witty, but occasionally profane language of an East Ender (as in Tower Hamlets) the articulate, demanding and sometimes peevish accents of the middle classes (Muswell Hill) or the rhythmic and musical patois of Caribbean people (Haringey) and finally the imperious, haughtiness of those residing in the Embassies (Kensington and Chelsea). Somewhere, at some point, the London social worker will encounter all human life. And it's fair to say, since I've worked in all of four of these boroughs, I speak with some authority.

I like social workers. Sometimes they have a bad press but the work is exceptionally tough and requires certain qualities not generally found among most sectors of the population. Endless patience, an interest in people beyond the norm, optimism, and compassion are part of the job description. All these might be seen as the virtues of a saint. Some social workers have all four of these qualities, some less, and some once may have possessed such qualities, but over time 'burn out.' Also known as 'compassion fatigue', it's the consequence of struggling with the endless and mindless bureaucracy which, together with the lack of resources, means eventually social workers reach a stage of exhaustion, and leave the profession.

There are two further and necessary qualities to social work; a sense of humour and a healthy dose of scepticism, if not cynicism. Although not usually advocated as either necessary or desirable in the average social work textbook, they're certainly essential. Being offered a mug of tea and watching an energetic flea jumping about without commenting on this, is a test of tolerance, as is accepting without refusal, tea boiled in a saucepan with several teaspoons of condensed milk routinely added to the mug. Or taking calls or visits to the office from the same person every day and several times a day, who is so obsessively anxious they cannot hold information for much longer than an hour or two; this too is an extreme test of tolerance.

Scepticism or even cynicism, although not generally advocated as beneficial to life in any type of work, with the exception of the police force, is sometimes necessary in social work. Note also, compassion is to some extent quite different—if not in opposition—to scepticism, which in the case of child abuse has led to miscarriages of justice. Here are a couple of examples which illustrate why at the very least scepticism is essential.

A small baby is found with a significant swelling on his head. The parents express somewhat unconvincingly with what appears to be distress and 'explain' that he climbed out of his high chair and fell on his head. Since he can barely sit up, this is highly unlikely but to suggest otherwise results in a verbal barrage, a torpedo of words designed to intimidate the social worker, who, for the sake of the baby's safety is trying to arrive at a truth.

Or take the case of an adolescent girl; in court for being 'beyond care and control', the legal term in use at the time. Standing by the bright lights of Marble Arch, her fourteen year old body is up for sale. She receives money and drugs in exchange for a 'freedom', the perverse and sexually gratifying use by others of her body and soul. Obviously, something has gone badly wrong in her childhood but this remains hidden. Both outside the court and within the court, she promises fervently she will cooperate with the magistrates, her parents' concerns, and myself as her social worker. All the time, while everyone knows that this may be her intention, she won't or can't, for any number of reasons.

I could go on, but whoever coined the phrase, 'the definition of a cynic is a disappointed idealist' was spot on. No matter how idealistic; scepticism and disbelief in social work keeps one in touch with reality and is a necessary shield against the gradual but inevitable feelings of disappointment.

Idealism is certainly one of the driving motivations for becoming a social worker but there are more hidden and more personal reasons. Understanding what these may be, came for myself later through psychotherapy. It was the moment when I realised that my own feelings of anger, depression, confusion and loss were often mirrored by the experiences of many social work clients. Still, despite this, or and perhaps because of this, I wanted to help others, but I didn't quite know how. I knew a little, that being rich or being poor didn't really explain how bad a person might feel, and there is more to understanding why people get depressed than how much money they owned or how materially secure or impoverished they were.

But there was something more; my primary motivation, and perhaps personal to me, had been to understand a client's psychological needs and to respond, hopefully appropriately and empathically. In other words, by helping others, I was helping myself. Ultimately, although perhaps a worthy and fairly innocent motivation, this need was destined to be unmet. And over time I began to see there was also a hidden aspect to social work.

At its heart, social work is political. By which I mean it incorporates issues of power, and not in a good way. Acting as a surrogate advocate, an activist, an accountant, a counsellor, all the time fighting for the rights of a client who is possibly and probably exhausted and angered by an uncaring and materially deprived system, makes one aware of this.

The state of welfare with its numerous laws and regulations, actively and passively contributes to the status quo of the system. Its driving motivation (hidden) is not therefore the welfare of a child or an individual, but cost and the stability of the political economy, whether local or national. Therefore it's not primarily the compassion of society that drives social work, but rather the passion of the accountant, which is an oxymoron in itself.

So while my intention here is not to write a political treatise, I eventually came round to the realisation that the practice of social work rests on a massive contradiction; that is the power and ultimate success of a political system ultimately is derived from the ownership of capital (So far, so obvious). Furthermore the Welfare State is a misnomer, since the term conceals a truth, this being the appearance of care but in reality it is used as a financial backup to a failing political economy. Therefore a social worker may start out with the best of intentions, but eventually they are confronted with this harsh reality.

These are important factors in the history of the Welfare State, but rarely are they explicitly acknowledged. But as far back as the eighteenth century, the philosopher and economist Adam Smith recognised this. In his classic analysis of society, the 'Theory of Moral Sentiments' he argued that the selfish interest of individuals (to make money) in the final analysis were harnessed for the 'public good'. He called this 'the hidden hand of capitalism.' He may well be right (partially) but this was not how I saw it. I did not privilege money but rather people and herein lies a contradiction. The Welfare State deals with symptoms, not the causes, which is why social workers are fundamentally faced with an impossible task.

For example, working as a social worker, in particular in the arena of mental health and child care, it became apparent that often, beyond the problems of financial insecurity, inadequate housing, insufficient medical care, a deprived education, and perhaps because of these, is an urgent need to form relationships, within which care and understanding could develop. But this takes time, and under the present system time equals money and within social work, time was, and still is, an intangible and elusive commodity. The following incidents out of many similar, left a lasting impression on me.

In one, I was to visit a young Muslim woman with severe mental health problems. She lived alone in a block of high rise flats in West London. It was so high that when the winds blew, the flat seemed to sway and the windows rattle. Thinking about this now, her fragility, her life experiences, and the uncertainty of who she was had developed partly out of her material circumstances.

Environments matter and often reflect dynamically the psyche of those who live in them. To reach her, I had to negotiate my way through the random network of streets and cul-de-sacs which then and now, starkly represents the deprivation and neglect of many social housing estates across Britain. Street signs were often defaced, cars vandalised, and graffiti sprayed along walls and the sides of buildings. The lift to her flat was scrawled with tags and smelt of urine and as it juddered up to eighth floor, I prayed it wouldn't break down.

On my first visit, she had asked me to remove my shoes before entering her flat, and after I had sat down and asked how she was, her eyes filled with tears. She told me with a voice shaking with emotion how much she disliked the medication prescribed for her. 'I live in a world surrounded by cotton wool' she said, 'there is no colour or sound.'

She was married, an arranged marriage, but she rarely saw her husband who was a medical student, his family still living back in Pakistan. The plan was to eventually return. Meanwhile, she lived without friends or family. Isolated in a high rise flat with only the view of the constant stream of traffic travelling along the West

London flyover to remind her there was a world outside. She lived a life of isolation in a virtual citadel, her descent into depression and medication wholly understandable. I knew what might help her, but I had neither the time nor did I have access to the necessary resources, if they existed.

Another occasion: I had been offered the opportunity to attend as witness to a 'family therapy' session. I had no previous knowledge of family therapy, or of the family, which consisted of the two parents and two children, a boy aged eight and a girl aged eleven. The girl's behaviour had become challenging and volatile. She was missing school and recently told her social worker her father was sexually abusing her. The parents had not been given this information, because the girl found the thought of communicating this secret, unsurprisingly unbearable. Consequently, it was thought by the managers that a meeting with the whole family might be useful.

Myself, the social worker for the family and her manager were placed behind a one way screen as observers. The family therapists started gently enough but were met with a hostile and unrelenting silence from all family members. This had the effect on the male therapist of making him increasingly direct, if not aggressive in his comments. It was at the point the young girl was challenged to tell her parents what she had told her social worker, that the session broke down.

Springing up from her chair she rushed out of the room, followed by the family therapist who grabbed her and forcibly attempted to drag her back. The girl became increasingly hysterical, and shouting and sobbing with distress, refused to return.

This incident put me off 'family therapy' for ever, although I was told often enough this experience was rare. The brutality of the therapist's intervention, the gross insensitivity to the young girl's experience, the indifference and ignorance of the power differential within the family, had a profound impact on me.

But this was not an isolated event. Another time, I witnessed a family brought together by the decision to 'section' their daughter. Faced with the combined forces of Welfare State; the doctor, the psychiatrist, a police officer, myself as social worker, I remember thinking, surely locking up one member identified as 'mad' is no solution. And I remember also thinking, that such experiences were profoundly distressing—especially for the one identified psychologically as 'mad.' But I had no power and felt I had to remain silent.

Such experiences gradually alerted me to the low status and lack of understanding of those categorised as mentally ill or emotionally troubled. They are seen as 'different' from the rest of society and once diagnosed, they may be written off and stigmatised, or seen as incapable of living an independent life. The release in 1975 of a film called, *One Flew Over the Cuckoo's Nest* only heightened my sensitivity to their plight (see Chapter 11). The film confirmed my growing disillusionment with social work particularly those classified as mentally ill. Social workers are faced on a daily basis with impossible tasks, yet were subjected to regular, ill-informed attacks by the press.

This injustice reminded me in some ways of my childhood, where assumptions had also been made about my character, intention, and of course, intelligence. Social workers were seen as stupid, naïve, and inappropriately 'political'. I questioned why we were seen with such hostility and finding it increasingly difficult to work in such a negative and unforgiving environment, I eventually began looking for a 'way out. I'd had enough. I also realised I lacked the necessary resilience for the work.

One day, while talking about these issues with a colleague, she told me she was 'in therapy'. This was new to me. She said she found psychotherapy helpful in all sorts of ways. I was intrigued. I began my research. I discovered psychotherapy offered an alternative way to understanding emotional troubles. It was not victim blaming. Its approach was profoundly personal, but at the same time there was a recognition of the power of families and societal structures which both constrains and demands a certain conformity of thought and behaviour.

In its place, was the possibility of freedom to think and feel with clarity. In other words, authenticity and honesty replaced ideology. I also realised that most, if not all psychotherapists express a basic humanitarianism in unravelling with a patient the historical and personal factors in an individual's confusion and distress. And above all, the fascinating ideal that, in particular, analytic psychotherapy had no formal agenda. This realisation was profoundly liberating. Eventually I found my own therapist and began an exploration of my own history. The experience of talking on a regular basis with someone who listened, without prejudice or judgement, was to become a turning point in my life.

— CHAPTER 10 —

Finding my Self

Carl Jung once wrote 'Who looks outside, dreams, who looks inside, awakes.'[10] With some trepidation and bearing Jung's observations in mind, I was about to experience my first session of psychotherapy. I had no idea what to expect.

We sit in diagonally placed chairs;. that way we could avoid looking at each other. Intentional? Probably. He was silent, calm, serious, and other than greeting me, said nothing further. I glance out of the window. It was one of those tall windows that led out onto a Juliet Balcony and I could see the neat garden that lay below. I turn towards him and without thinking too much, I said, 'I'm wondering what theories you follow?'

He could have put the question back to me. He could have said, 'What theories do you think I might follow?' or, 'I'm wondering why you ask that question?' but he said neither. His answer was straightforward and direct, 'We'll find out'. His response impressed me. The implication of a joint venture was attractive. I liked his response

---

10   Carl Jung, 'Letter to Fanny Bowditch', 1916.

and I liked him. For the next four years we met on a regular basis. For the next four years I began to make sense of my life.

We met weekly in a small room on the first floor of a tall, terraced white house overlooking the well-maintained garden. It was kept locked. Time passed; I became aware that I wanted to sit in that garden on a particular bench. It was placed in the far corner. It was Victorian with decorative cast iron ends and a slatted oak seat which had turned grey with age. Eventually, Instead of sitting in my car waiting for my session, I suggested to him that I would wait on that bench.

His reply? 'I know it's important to you, but it's not my garden, therefore, I'm sorry but you'll have to wait as usual until I can see you.' I felt both irritated and disappointed, but said nothing. Eventually I was to discover why the garden held so much appeal for me and why this was especially true in the spring. Then the garden would come alive and slowly unfurl from its bare, frozen existence and the cold repressions of winter. It was coming alive, and at such times, and before my session, I would peer through the black painted ornate railings at the lawn and the surrounding plants and flowers.

In the spring, the garden had a certain ambience about it. An otherworldliness of grace and an elegance and even though it was an urban garden, it seemed to belong to another era, another place. The lawn was surrounded by a hedge of sweet smelling orange blossom, tall verbena, and the deep purple flower of the lilac. The flowers were carelessly abundant, their colours defiantly white and purple against the drab buildings in the background and seeing them filled me with joy. Their growth was magical; their presence so close to the mayhem of London traffic that the garden seemed like an oasis, representing calmness and predictability. Yet understanding its personal significance came later and only after I had sat and talked for some months in his drab, understated room.

Having his total attention for fifty minutes had given me the freedom, the space to talk about anything. Anything. Anything which came to my mind. There was no agenda other than my own. I began speaking out about the past, and of those times when I hadn't fitted in and felt rejected and excluded. I told him about my accident and how my mother had remarried as soon as I'd left the hospital and how I was taken to another city and how for two years we lived with her parents-in-law. I told him how they resented my presence, that they knew nothing about me, asked nothing of me. I was of no consequence. Invisible, I was condemned to silence. I was displaced. A child with no past.

I felt as an alien, a wild child, with no roots, and no attachments. I asked myself, was I wild? A child of nature? Was I angry? Yes, I was angry, I said, of course I was angry, wouldn't you be? I was bereft, in pain, an emotional pain which tore me apart. I missed the care of my aunt's and uncle's love and affection and even though I had prayed, as my aunt had suggested, that one day I would return to them, my prayers had gone unanswered. I was alone and lost. For years I had dreamt of a dark tidal wave submerging me. At night I had lain awake, frightened of falling asleep and drowning in a vale of tears.

Now all those years later, the garden evoked feelings of being shut out. It seemed so attractive, but someone else had the keys and I wasn't wanted. Once again, I felt unacceptable and as if there was something wrong with me. The garden represented what might have been my childhood, the keys the prison guards of my past and of my mind.

When I'd first began therapy, I'd hardly been aware of these memories. I'd protected myself by pushing them to the back of my mind and therefore I couldn't have known of them or spoken of them. But now I had the freedom to think and talk about anything and everything and although this made the experience sometimes painful, it felt liberating, beguiling, not to say fascinating.

That garden and my therapy were transforming my feelings. My sessions came to represent the calm and peace I had lacked as a child and the regular sessions with my therapist were representative of the acceptance and the psychic growth I needed. He was a witness. A translator of the past, an interpreter for the present. His voice quiet. He said very little, asked few questions, but he listened, and remembered without prompting whatever I told him. He was totally reliable and totally serious. I could rely on the predictability of a response. He seemed without moods and whatever I threw at him, whether provocative, angry or tearful, received the same careful attention and understanding.

These sessions were the beginning of my love affair with analytic psychotherapy. Before long my preoccupation was in full swing. I felt as if I belonged to a rare clique, one with a special language, which used strange concepts and unfamiliar words. At parties, the cognoscenti i.e. those 'in therapy' would form a small group and swop stories about 'being in therapy.' 'What did we talk about before?' No one knew or cared. Now we had an endless source of fascinating material we shared with others like ourselves. The material was life, our own lived experiences, an oral history, which gave shape and meaning to formless and disconnected experiences, and in that long process we found ourselves.

I'd been a late starter, or that's how it seemed. Once I'd left home, I'd become academically successful, with a doctorate in Critical Theory. Gained while working as a social worker, I was already drawn to the angry, the depressed, the confused, and the dispossessed. In some ways, I saw in them a reflection of myself and I wanted to understand how we or they came to be like that. I also wanted to help, but I didn't know how. I knew a little, that being rich or being poor didn't really explain how bad a person might feel, and that there was more to understanding why people got depressed than how much money they owned or how materially secure they were. I also knew thinking and feeling were different states of mind. Separated they could be disastrous, but bring them together and something creative and even liberating could happen.

Gradually I came to the conclusion that analytic psychotherapy was a way of life which fascinated me. It required an ability to think and work in different ways. The language, the concepts and the values of psychotherapy, I now knew from personal experience worked.

I no longer teetered along the edge of despair, or would think of myself with self-loathing, or simmer with repressed anger at a real or imagined slight. Not that I had transformed into someone else, but something durable and real had developed through talking all that time in the room on the first floor in Islington. Someone who was prepared to listen and understand in some obscure way had changed how I felt and thought about myself.

I now knew myself, I could make sense of who I was, and understand why I felt or thought in the way I did. I could link feelings and thoughts with events and understand what was really important, and now I had the words to say how I felt. Thinking and feeling had become one. I also had realised that while a therapy session seemed to consist only in listening and talking, it was far more than a 'chat'.

Any comment, any conversation, any reported event or happening, had two levels of understanding. One was the literal, the real event, the other was a metaphor. Both were important, but the metaphor could hold the truth to what was really going on.

It wasn't a difficult decision resolving to train as an analytic psychotherapist. I began researching into the different analytic training programmes. There were plenty to choose from. My work as a social worker in deprived areas of London and my background in sociology had made me sensitive to the tone and content of the different training programmes. Anything that smacked of elitism, superiority, self-importance was out. Anything that indicated a certain superficiality in the process of training was out. Anything that implied the possibility of easy financial success was also out. Politically I was left of centre and against materialism, and appeals to making money at the expense of someone's distress grated with me. Neither did I want to advise or solve anybody's problems. For me, life didn't work that way.

It took a while to know what I was looking for, but eventually I found it. The organisation was the Arbours Association. I'd heard of Arbours from various friends. It was based in Crouch End, not so far from my own therapy in Islington. Its radical reputation, its critique of the usual concepts of mental illness, its Communities, the Crisis Centre, all held a fascination for me and I wanted to be part of it.

Once I had looked out of the window, beyond the building and the garden where I met for my therapy, I could see a major thoroughfare.. It was just about visible from where I stood. Usually choked with the noisy rabble of London traffic, the road curved past Highbury Corner Tube and continued up the Holloway Road until eventually it reached Archway and Highgate. At the junction where Waitrose stood, instead of continuing straight ahead, I could turn left for Tufnell Park, or right for Finsbury Park and if I did this, after a twenty minute walk, passing first under the Railway Bridge, then up and over the hill, I would have reached Crouch End. Alternatively I could catch a bus.

And that's where I wanted to be, leafy, middle class and affluent, Crouch End in North London was and still is a desirable place to live. In the spring the streets are lined with the blossom of cherry trees, making a delicate contrast with the tall, red brick Victorian houses, standing three or four stories high. Some had retained their art nouveau balconies, and some had been converted into flats, which were rented or owned by those working in the City or the West End. The shops were of the type usually favoured by the successful and educated; high end supermarkets, quality greengrocers, delicatessens, themed restaurants and expensive, designer style cafes.

All this implies a life style based on predictability and conformity, at least as far as appearance goes, but the fact was, there was another part of Crouch End which was anything but respectable or conforming. It was the part of London which provides the background to this story because from the 1970s through to the present time, Crouch End was also the home to the Arbours Association, a unique organisation and one of the most progressive and committed therapeutic organisations of its time.

From the 1970s Arbours established and ran three therapeutic Communities and a Crisis Centre, which meant for those in the know, it becoming known as 'Couch End'. The Crisis Centre provided a haven for those seen as psychologically extremely vulnerable, while the Community houses were intended for people with a history of long term and disabling emotional problems. Both places gave residents an opportunity to share their lives with similar others.

Most often they were self-referrals, and financed privately or by Social Security. The fact that they were called residents, and not patients, removed to some extent the stigma associated with hospitals and psychiatry. While living in a community they received intensive and varied forms of therapy. Apart from dance, art, group and individual psychotherapy, an important part of their lives, was the experience of living together on a day-to-day basis.

My decision was fast. I was confident that choosing Arbours for my training was the right decision. Their work and ideas were progressive, but also representative of the times. The zeitgeist was liberating, optimistic and creative. Fashion, music and design buzzed with innovation, that was for some. Yet for the many who worked with the emotionally troubled, there was a dissatisfaction with popular ideas about mental health. The surrealists in Continental Europe from the 1930s had played with Freud's ideas of the unconscious and psychoanalysis and had linked them with ideas of emancipation and creativity, yet therapeutic work on the explicit basis of such values had yet to develop.

The Arbours Association and the similar Philadelphia Organisation were however about to change this. In London, New York and other cities of America, many were turning to psychoanalytic psychotherapy to make sense of their lives. It was from within this group came the ideas for a different way of working with the emotionally troubled.

Once I had heard of Arbours, I had little interest in other trainings. I submitted an application and waited with some apprehension and excitement for my interview. I remember that day clearly. I made my way with some trepidation to the address I'd been given.

My interviewer lived in one of those tall Crouch End houses I found so attractive. His room was at the top of the house and was full of interest. I glanced round. There was a sense of warmth and calmness. The lighting was subdued, the walls were lined with books, many of which related to analysis and psychotherapy, including, I seem to remember, the complete works of Freud. I was mightily impressed.

I sat down in one of the chairs and glanced round. There was another chair that looked like it might be French but it was definitely vintage. It reminded me of a similar one I'd seen once in a Bloomsbury antique shop. The large feather filled cushion was covered with an orange, blue, and rust covered kilim, while the sides and the back of the chair consisted of intricately woven cane. A rug hung on the wall. But just as I was wondering whether it was Turkish or Afghan, my interviewer began to speak. He had a directness, an intensity, a seriousness about him which I found at first slightly disconcerting. There was no small talk.

He asked first about my therapy. I'd expected that question. I was prepared for it.

'It transformed me' I said, adding, 'and my view of the world'. He put his head on one side as if to ask a question or make a comment but thought better of it, because he remained silent. I continued, 'I mean, things and people are rarely what they seem … at least that's what I think.'

'So what does that mean to you?'

'It means … it means I couldn't trust people, or not at first. I'd think, do they mean what they say, or say what they mean?'

'So honesty and directness are important to you.'

I nodded. Despite his seriousness, he intuitively knew how to put me at my ease. The style of his questioning proceeded like a therapeutic encounter; calm, thoughtful, reflectively slow, with a capacity to tolerate silence. He moved on, asking more about myself, my childhood, my friendships, my work, but to each of these, he made no further comment to my response.

The interview, I remember, seemed to passed quickly but as we came to an end, he said, 'I've told you a little about Arbours. The work is challenging. Can you tell me why you want to train as a psychotherapist?'

My answer sounded banal. Why would I want to train as a therapist? I wished then that I had an amazingly insightful response to this question but I hadn't, so instead I said, 'That's a deceptively straightforward question … but I have thought about it. I guess I want to help others, particularly those labelled as mentally ill. I've worked as a social worker and I've noticed the system is stacked against those who don't conform. I've seen relatives turn against members of their own family and it's too easy to get a patient sectioned and the consequences are inevitably serious.'

I continued, 'and besides that, there's personal reasons. I've been in therapy for a while … and it's been a good experience.'

'And?'

'And … that's all I want to say right now.' I wanted to avoid talking about the accident and my childhood which might have meant opening 'Pandora's Box' so I smiled in what I hoped was a disarming way.

He said, 'It sounds as if your therapy has been important to you. Would you say that others could benefit from a similar experience?'

'Yes, definitely. I would say many, if not most. It was and still is important to me.'

'Well, you may know that ideally we require our trainees to have had substantial experience of their own psychotherapy before they start and it's essential this continues throughout the training. Would that be a problem for you?'

'Not at all.'

Other than to glance at his watch briefly he didn't react, but as we were about to finish, he asked if I had any further questions. With some hesitation and nervousness, I aske, 'I was wondering what attitude Arbours takes in the use of drugs for those suffering a mental illness?'

There was a short pause before he replied, 'We believe in using the therapeutic relationship to help and care for the troubles a patient may experience.'

This for me, was the perfect response. Not only had he avoided making a reference to any medical diagnosis and the use of medication, but reassuringly, he had confirmed the potential power of psychotherapy. Following that interview, for the next five years, I became totally preoccupied with achieving that aim.

— CHAPTER 11 —

The Radical Heart of the Arbours Association

In 1975 the film called *One Flew Over the Cuckoo's Nest* was released. Based on the book of the same name, the film is now recognised as an iconic and powerful commentary on mental illness. Set in a psychiatric hospital in the state of Oregon, in the USA, it portrays the tragic downfall of a patient by the name of McMurphy.

Played by Jack Nicholson, McMurphy seeks to avoid the consequences of a rape conviction by getting himself admitted to an acute psychiatric hospital for an assessment. Here he is confronted with behaviour which can only be understood as a response to the extreme control and discipline of a psychiatric hospital, to which we can add the harmful effects of medication. Despite many patients being resident on a voluntary basis, they exhibit a range of bizarre behaviour: facial tics, robotic and repetitive movements of the body, and one in choosing as his defence, 'elective mutism' effectively has removed himself from all verbal communication.

In contrast to these scenes of institutionalised insanity, McMurphy bursts on the scene with a bravado performance of outrage. Motivated by energy, fear, anger, and clearly bewildered and enraged by what he observes, his opposition to the ward's repressive regimes becomes more extreme. In response, he is confronted with the unmitigated force and disapproval of the senior nurse, Nurse Ratched. If McMurphy represents anarchy and disorder, Nurse Ratched epitomises control and authoritarianism. She has developed to a fine art the sadism which inhabits her soul as shown by the ice cold, blue-eyed stare by which she controls the patients on her ward.

Kirk Douglas, the well-known Hollywood actor, director and author who died in 2020, was so moved by this account of institutionalised madness that he fought long and hard to make the film. It carried a message many preferred to avoid. The problems were many; the funding, the acting, the script. Eventually, ten years on the film received the recognition it deserved. It was nominated for numerous awards, with a particular recognition for the roles of McMurphy and Ratched, both of which were seen as outstanding portrayals of madness.

In terms of the film's message, its anti-authoritarianism and advocacy for the 'underdog', the film can be understood as a vivid representation of the spirit of the times. For years there had been global protests against the American involvement in the Vietnam war. At the same time, evidence was accumulating on 'post-traumatic stress syndrome', the long term effects of war on the shattered body and minds of returning soldiers. And running parallel with these protests, was the growing dissatisfaction, if not rejection, of popular ideas about mental health.

Evidence emanating from Freudian scholars and other psychoanalysts pointed to the importance of the 'real event' which together with the influence of the concept of the unconscious via dreams and phantasies, suggested alternative explanations. It was argued that mental illness could be understood as an existential problem and the consequence of distorted relationships.

Yet Freud's notion of the 'unconscious' paradoxically, could also be seen as a source for emancipation and creativity. For example, from the 1930s the 'surrealists' in continental Europe, whether artists, photographers, political activists or philosophers, recognised its potential for political and personal freedom. The politicisation of what was seen originally as an interesting but eccentric viewpoint of a privileged intellectual elite, was gradually becoming more influential. Interpreting society though the lens of Freud's theory of repression pointed to new ways of understanding personal and social breakdown, and nowhere was this more evident than in the writings of the Frankfurt School.

Originating in the universities of Germany it became known as 'Critical Theory'. The authors, radical sociologists, philosophers, psychologists and political scientists, in analysing and searching for some form of explanation for the horrific rise of Nazism and the death camps of the Holocaust, explicitly linked Marxism with psychoanalysis as providing a possible framework of interpretation. Their success in 'deconstructing' the ideology of capitalism with its supposed objectivity based on the 'facts' of empirical evidence, was such they were forced to flee from the murderous rule of the Nazis. Subsequently they settled in the cities of London, New York, and Paris from where their influence grew steadily. They argued that pain and suffering was related to the structure of society and that understanding this, necessarily preceded any emancipation and enlightenment.

As one of the major proponents of Critical Theory, Adorno's work on the 'authoritarian personality 'was particularly relevant.[11] The roots of fascism, he argued, lay in privileging dominating and irrational forms of law and order, as shown by its opposition to ideas and forms of intellectualism, and its contempt for subjectivity of whatever kind, including that of art.

The influence of extreme authoritarianism had long been associated as a cause of mental illness. Back in 1945, Wilhelm Reich in his book, *Listen, Little Man* argued passionately for the freedom

11 Theodor Adorno et al., *The Authoritarian Personality*, Harper, 1950.

of the spirit and the soul, seeing its repression as a cause of the rise of fascism. A film released in 2009, many years later and after *One Flew Over the Cuckoo's Nest* addresses these issues. Shot in black and white *The White Ribbon* written and directed by the Austrian film director, Michael Haneke, tells the story of early twentieth century life in a small village in North Germany. Haneke states the film is about the origins of evil, whether religious or political terrorism. 'They're both the same' he says.

Thus the film brilliantly creates an atmosphere of extreme control and disapproval towards children who fail to conform, an ideology which subsequently legitimised the sadistic punishment meted out to them by parents and teachers.

Yet, despite these early efforts to repress psychoanalysis, its ideas and influence continued to spread. This was particularly true of the urban populations of the West, but also included certain cities such as in Argentina and Latin America where psychoanalysis was gradually seen as a politically liberating force. By the 1960s, many had turned to psychoanalytic psychotherapy to make sense of their lives and it was from within these groups that the ideas for a different way of working with mental illness developed.

The Arbours Association was one such group. As an organisation, with its roots based in east and then north London, it soon became known not only for its radical thinking on mental illness, but also for its development of progressive forms of analytic psychotherapy. Its psychotherapists worked for a more enlightened therapy, specifically in relation to their commitment to analytic work with the more severely emotionally troubled.

Founded in the 1970s by two American doctors, Dr Joe Berke and the psychiatrist, Dr Morten Schatzman, Arbours was based on a foundation of progressive and democratic ideas of openness. This, together with a well-developed critique of the institutionalisation of the mentally ill, sought to provide an alternative to the then current psychiatric treatment for severely distressed individuals.

Both Joe Berke and Morty Schatzman were originally medically trained in New York but once qualified, left the States to live in London and to meet with, amongst others, the Glaswegian psychiatrist, R.D. Laing. Their approach to the work was complimentary. Dr Joseph Burke was outspoken, flamboyant, sometimes outrageously provocative, Dr Morton Schatzman, the quieter, more considered and intellectual of the two. As a team they worked well. Their friendship had continued after they moved to London, which meant together with R.D. Laing and others who shared their vision, the Arbours Association, based on the ideas of an alternative therapeutic organisation gradually took shape.

R.D. Laing, was a fierce advocate and interpreter of the mentally troubled. His writing was powerful, poetic and authentic, his voice more philosophical than psychiatric. 'Going mad' was understood as a process, as potentially creative, imbued with the capacity to see the truth. This included an awareness of the many concessions and psychic adjustments the sane feel obliged to make every day. For Laing, madness and sanity are dynamic concepts, psychically transformative, its expression potentially changing from hour to hour. These are not binary state of minds; the mad are also sane, and the sane contain always their own disavowed craziness.

He observed that with patients who fear they are mad, are suicidal, or complain of feeling depressed, that such complaints are not meaningless or specific to that particular patient. In the background the original instigators of such disturbances remain silent and apparently uninvolved, and understanding their influence was always part of any therapy.

Laing had noted the potential complexity and subtly of statements which may occur within any conversation. Statements might be disclaimed (denied), avowed (but not admitted), contradicted (yet with no realisation of an opposite) or contain a paradox, (an absurdity). He argued that how such statements are made is equally important to what is being said. Thus, innuendoes, tone of voice, facial expressions and gestures are also capable of expressing an alternative meaning to the actual words.

Equally destructive are communications based on an inherent contradiction. Here, there is no possibility of getting anything right. Laing, drawing on the work of Gregory Bateson, an anthropologist and social scientist who developed the concept of the 'double-bind', stipulated the following characteristics.. These being an audience, a particular type of communication which is repeated, that the communication may take the form of a gesture, facial expression, or tone of voice, and finally that the first communication may be followed by a second, which directly contradicts the first.

This is the essence of the 'double bind' ass illustrated by the following typical interaction. The imagined conversation occurs between a mother, her daughter and the mother's friend and is based on a number of different accounts which patients have relayed to me over the years.

B, a patient, tells me of the following conversation between herself, her mother (A) and her mother's friend (C) as they sit one morning in the kitchen.

B has often said somehow her mother 'puts her down' and psychically ties her in knots, but she cannot understand how this happens. Bear in mind all conversations within a family hold a particular history, a repetition of how people relate to each other.

The conversation begins when A says to B, 'You said you enjoy baking, so why don't you make that carrot cake you said you like.' (Implication that while B says she likes to make and eat the carrot cake, A does not, and the tone, 'you said you liked' also implies some doubt. Why not, 'you like.')

Without waiting for an answer, A then turns to C, raises her eyes to the ceiling, stands back with her arms folded, then looking directly at B says, 'Do you know if you have all the ingredients?' (Implication here that A is competent whereas B is both incompetent and forgetful).

B says, 'I'll check it out.' She begins to look in the cupboard, at which point A pushes past her and says, 'Here let me look.' (The implication A is efficient and knows what is needed, unlike B).

'Over her shoulder' A says to C, 'She tries but she needs me to help her. I don't know what she'd do without me.' (Here she invites

C to join her in putting down B as if she is a child, at the same time as excluding B). B tells me at this point she felt confused.

C nods her head but makes no comment possibly because she finds herself drawn into a strange dynamic.

A continues, she says, 'Anyway, it's usually easier if I make it. I know what I'm doing.' (A is denying B's ability to cook by implying that B can only survive with A's support).

So here, in a fairly short conversation, what has been demonstrated is that despite the apparent appearance of kindness, in A offering to help B, in reality the opposite is true. B has been faced with a number of implicit critical attributions undermining her competence, her independence, and her sense of self.

Quoting Bateson, Laing writes that this type of communication when repeated constantly, inevitably results in an individual finding it difficult to feel sane with an awareness of who they are and what they want. In the above situation, A has conveyed to B what she could do, but on another level that she should not or cannot because she is personally incapable of fulfilling the identified task. In this dynamic B's freedom to act has been blocked by A attributing to her a number of thoughts and actions that actually belong to A. From this interaction, B's sense of self has been undermined.

Whereas much of Laing's therapeutic work took place in London and Glasgow, in the United States, psychiatrists and analysts such as Harold Searles, were also contributing to these observations and debates. Within psychiatry, he was seen as an outsider. Reportedly, many of his academic papers were rejected, possibly because his work was highly original since he also included the role of the therapist in any interpretation as in the following.

In one of his most well-known papers, called 'The Patient as Therapist to his Analyst', he commented that the more ill the patient, the more that successful treatment relies on an implicit assumption that the patient is also the analyst's therapist.[12] A profound observation that recognises both the therapist and the

---

12 Harold Searles, 'The Patient as Therapist to his Analyst In *Tactics and Techniques in Psychoanalytic Theory* P. Giovacchini, ed. Jason Aronson Inc, 1975.

patient share a common understanding of the emotional foundations to suffering and that, individually, each are part of a 'therapeutic symbiosis'. There is in this, a recognition that the 'self' and 'other' are part of a mutual relationship in how the world is experienced and perceived.

In another of his papers, 'The Effort to Drive the Other Person Crazy', Searles makes a similar point to Laing's observation on the culture of particular families.[13] Here there is the communication of both a covert and overt expression of hostility towards an identified family member. The consequence of such attitudes is that he or she will eventually feel mad but also be regarded as schizophrenic. He cites one of his patients as commenting to him about her family of origin, 'Murder, that's wrong but there's other ways.' Searles' argument is that within some families, there is a long standing unconscious effort to drive another member crazy.

This also is an example of Becker and Goffman's theories on 'mystification' (the role of confusing the other by a 'performance'. To be successful, there must be a power imbalance. This exploits differences of status, age, education etc., therefore behaviour must be subtle, convincing, disorientating, and hidden. Mystification, in particular has entered the national psyche and is now called 'gaslighting' after the film *Gaslight*. Released in 1944, the story focuses on a newly married couple, the protagonist played by Charles Boyer with Ingrid Bergman as the victim is a powerful evocation of the destructive manipulation of the mind.

Searles died in 2015 aged 97, but left behind a body of work significant for its compassion and understanding. He worked analytically for many years with those seen as 'borderline' and 'schizophrenic' during which, at the same time, in London, the anti-psychiatry movement continued to develop.

Morty Schatzman, Joe Berke and R.D. Laing were to become a major part of this scene in London. Profoundly compassionate

---

13 Harold Searles, 'The Effort to Drive the Other Person Crazy: An Element in the Aetiology and Psychotherapy of Schizophrenia', *British Journal of Medical Psychology*, Vol 32(1): 1–18, 1959.

and articulate defenders for the rights of the mentally ill, their work attracted a number of supporters who shared in their vision and who came from the similar backgrounds of psychology, social work, and psychiatry.

The organisational centre for these developments initially took place in Kingsley Hall. Based in London's East end, with its long history of radical community involvement, society was seen as oppressive, controlling, authoritarian, with the result many felt alienated. Psychiatry in particular was seen as 'society's cop'. The mentally troubled were portrayed as diseased and sick, which could mean being sectioned, locked up or subjected to a series of electric shocks, known as ECT, or electroconvulsive therapy.

Astonishingly, ECT is still used today, although the patient's consent is sought and broken bones caused by fits during this treatment, is now unlikely. Despite such reassurances, for many it remains a barbaric treatment.

Their opposition to how mental illness was understood (or not understood), how it was treated, and its underlying politics, was eventually documented in a book called *The Radical Therapist*. Published by Penguin in 1974, it contained a widespread critique of the ways in which society treats the 'mentally ill'. The book contains many views, but common to them all was the concern and compassion for those diagnosed as mentally ill. Both Joseph Berke and Morton Schatzman, as the founders of the Arbours Association were contributors.

The Radical Therapist was and still is a ground-breaking critique of the psychiatry.[14] In an article called 'Madness and Morals', Morty Schatzman wrote 'Lectures in psychiatry, anti-psychiatry, and phenomenology, and seminars and meetings with professional people in many fields occurred in Kingsley Hall. The community was a link in a chain of 'counter-culture' centres. Experimental drama groups, social scientists of the New Left, classes from the University of London, leaders of the commune movement, and avant-garde poets, artists, musicians, dancers and photographers,

---

14 The Radical Therapist Collective, *The Radical Therapist*. Penguin, 1974.

have met at Kingsley Hall with the residents. The Free School of London met there for the first time.'

In an interview with Joe Berke, (interviewer remained anonymous) he was asked how he understood insanity. He replied, insanity was a social phenomenon, and whether certain behaviour was classified as mad or not, depended upon cultural norms. He stressed that whatever the diagnosis, there was never an understanding of what the person might feel or what experiences they might have had.

He pointed out how the term schizophrenia was used in such a way to invalidate an individual's thoughts or behaviour. He saw insanity as a social and cultural experience and argued that a textbook definition doesn't or cannot explain or express how or what a person was feeling. Yet, as he pointed out, 'normal' people were likely to have experienced the same or similar thoughts at some point during their lives.

Essentially he saw madness as the outcome of a crazy society, and that people are tricked into thinking it's solely their problem and their fault, whereas, he argued, it is a social problem ultimately derived from distorted relationships.

Morty Schatzman shared Joe Berke's view. In 'Madness and Morals' he takes apart the ideology of the mental hospital. He writes as an impassioned and critical analysis of the psychiatric hospital. For example, he draws attention to a psychiatrist's use of medical language and how it confirms the power of psychiatry. Thus he sees the patient's examination as actually a 'trial,' a 'judgement', the outcome 'a sentence', and the 'correction' is actually 'treatment.'

Any protest by the patient is transformed by the psychiatrist into 'he's too ill to recognise he's ill.' The whole process, he observed was based on 'mystification.' The psychiatrist working within a typical mental hospital starts from this questionable premise that the patient fails to see that he is ill, but the patient doesn't recognise this, purely because he is ill. (A teleological, circular argument which is incapable of being tested.)

The prescription of a series of drugs, only exacerbates the patient's symptoms. As a consequence, the patient begins to feel paranoid and fearful of the hospital and the treatment. The staff interprets this as a sign of illness rather than as an understandable response to the coercive treatment they are forced to endure. Hence the mental hospital succeeds only in escalating a patient's fears of madness.

Citing Freud, Morty Schatzman points to an alternative way of making sense of a patient's life. Freud observed that in patients who had earlier experienced trauma, such experiences had been repressed. He encouraged patients to recover these forgotten memories and lost feelings as a way of becoming whole and understanding themselves. For an Arbours therapist, familiarity with both classical and modern analytic theory was pivotal in their training and this perspective went alongside a respect for the value, the autonomy, and the unique potential of each individual.

The importance of the mutual process of how people relate and talk to each other has also long been recognised by many poets and philosophers and found within their writing over the passage of time. For example, John Donne, the metaphysical poet of the sixteenth and seventeenth Centuries wrote, 'No man is an island entire of itself; every man is a piece of the continent,' and Karl Marx, writing in the nineteenth century observed, 'Men make their own history, but they do not make it just as they please; they do not make it under self-selected circumstances, but under circumstances existing already'.

And more recently, Donald Winnicott, a twentieth-century paediatrician and a psychoanalyst commented, 'When I think of a baby, I think of the mother,' meaning in the first months of a baby's life he or she is wholly dependent on the mother's care. The earlier and the more persistent an interaction between mother and child, the more likely the impact, whether good or bad, it may have. Some of these influences may be subtle, and some obvious, but for Winnicott they indicated the baby's relationship with the mother.

The intention in making such comments is to illustrate for the reader how certain analytic concepts inform the therapist's understanding and how these early influences may be reproduced when a patient feels troubled. At times, the psychotherapist may face the silence and pessimism of the depressed, the tears of the bereaved, the fears of the anxious, the anger and resentment of the victimised, the excitement of the ambitious. But whatever the history of a patient or the possible causes of their troubles, the psychotherapist's ultimate aim is to contain and make sense with the patient of such feelings.

Praxis

'The process of milieux therapy meant we were all on a steep learning curve. We learnt to observe facial expressions, that eyes can show pain, distress, anger, confusion, and blank eyes have meaning. There is no absence. Rather it's something masquerading as nothing. No-thing, no-body, no-sense, words which in this context carried the mystery of an underlying psychic trouble, not yet verbalised, not yet understood. We learnt to listen with care, with patience, sensitivity and compassion. To note the change of key, the change of tempo, the silence, the sigh, and worse, the cut-off, the closed-down, the tight lips, the eyes that spark with contempt, dislike, hostility indifference or disbelief. We observed them, noted them, and considered their meaning.'

— CHAPTER 12 —

Milieux Therapy in an Arbours Community

It was midsummer and I was standing outside one of the Communities, talking to my supervisor about my forthcoming placement. I'd asked him to explain 'milieux therapy.' He'd been non-committal and said it was up to me, that it varied from therapist to therapist, that there are no rules, but it was an opportunity for both the resident and the therapist to get to know each other.

'Surely there are some rules?' I'd said, to which he'd replied, 'Be friendly but not a friend, hold boundaries, don't disclose too much personal information, listen (without prejudice or judgement) and don't favour one more than another. In a nutshell he'd said, 'Just be there for them', and, he added, 'After they've met you, it's usual for them to hold a meeting and they'll decide then whether you can stay.'

Seeing my face, he said, 'Well, it is their home, you know. Don't worry, you'll be fine.'

'Fine.' I felt anything but fine.

Firstly, I was racked with the terror of being rejected and excluded. Had I known that fear before? Yes, but not to the same extent. Although I could reason with myself that I had had the experience as a social worker of working with the most angry, the most deprived, the most unreasonable who ever set foot on this planet, somehow this now paled into insignificance. I was aware I was about to be judged. The residents had the power to reject me.

Spending time on a daily basis with the residents in a Community for weeks or months, without the regular framework of a one-to-one framework, made this type of therapeutic work particularly demanding. From dawn to dusk, the intensity of relationships with the residents was woven into the fabric and the life of the community and all who lived there. It was the place where relationships, real and imagined were felt, experienced and verbalised. It was a cauldron of emotions, stirred with passion, affection, confusion, dislike and hostility. Avoiding this was unthinkable.

From the 1970s Arbours established and ran three Communities and a Crisis Centre and within each of these, milieux therapy was of fundamental importance. The Crisis Centre provided a haven for the extremely vulnerable, while the Community houses were intended for people with a history of long term, emotional problems. These gave residents an opportunity to share their lives with others while at the same time receiving other different types of psychotherapy, such as dance, art, and individual therapy.

The communities were central to the Arbours experience, and separated the training of an Arbours psychotherapist from that of others. Attention was given to the smallest detail. For example, many patients traumatised by a past clinical experience were particularly sensitive to the 'look' of their surroundings. They felt different but it was important that they felt 'merged in' with the general population. So within the Communities, they were called residents, and within the Crisis Centre they were called guests. By and large, they were there on a voluntary basis and could leave when they liked, although any vacancy was soon filled, as there was often a waiting list to become a resident.

Substantial and attractive, the Crouch End houses had large bay windows, some with a look of faded affluence. The hallways were often finished with decorative ceramic tiling. The front porch windows and door, in line with the ideas of the Arts and Crafts Movement, remained true to style and were glazed in emerald green, ruby red and cobalt blue glass. The residents had considerable freedom to contribute to their living spaces. Many were artistic and decorated the walls of their bedroom with their own paintings and designs.

Milieux therapy firstly, and perhaps obviously, depends upon an ability to put oneself in another's shoes. This requires a more or less immediate capacity to observe and recognise those who feel troubled and out of step with life's expectations, and follow through such observations with curiosity but without judgement. It is about making sense of the daily experience within a Community of living and talking together. In communicating an understanding, the therapist aims to clarify the thoughts and feelings the patient has indicated, but not yet articulated. This maybe because the patient is unaware of them or fears voicing them. Typically, the therapist says very little. The focus is on what has been said in the context of everything known about the patient.

Therapeutic listening was and is, not like a 'chat' or similar to a conversation with a friend, as occasionally I have heard it so described. The ability to listen without interruption is fundamental, since within any session, whether in the Community or in a one-to-one, a silence has both a potential to heal or to intrude. The term, 'breaking the silence' indicates that potential and the more fragile the patient the more important it is to get it right. In communicating an understanding of what the patient is saying, a therapist aims to clarify the thoughts and feelings the patient has indicated, but not yet articulated.

The process of milieux therapy meant we were all on a steep learning curve. We learnt how to observe facial expressions, how eyes can show pain, distress, anger, and confusion, and that blank eyes have meaning. There is no absence, rather it's something masquerading as nothing. No-thing, no-body. no-sense, all words which in this context, carry the mystery as to an underlying psychic trouble, not yet verbalised, not yet understood. We learnt to listen with care, with patience, sensitivity and compassion. To note the change of key, the change of tempo, the silence, the sigh, and worse, the cut-off, the closed-down, the tight lips, the eyes that spark with contempt, dislike, hostility. Indifference or disbelief, observe them, note them, and consider their meaning.

We learnt to listen to the sound of words. The soft whisper, or its opposite, where there is little modulation and noted how it felt and when it changed. And we listened to the tense, past or present, what might that mean? And the speed of delivery … was that an escape, was it running away, a verbal flight to avoid feeling?

And those long silences, together with the carefully chosen and occasional word? Was this a sign of trauma, of experiences that were unspeakable? Did the words lack meaning or significance? And were there constant interruptions; of themselves or of yourself? And how did that make us feel? Non-existent, insignificant, redundant?

Everything, every feeling, every action, every thought can work in different ways; and whether real or imagined, we struggled to understand them. It was an experience rich with surprising insights. It was in the Community, we were taught not to hide, to stay with difficulties, to be direct, speak the truth, and accept that even when the story was bizarre, we were to discover, everything has some meaning. This may take time to understand, but despite this, it was worth the effort. We learnt that the form of every communication tells its own story, and this is as important as the content.

What follows are three accounts of everyday life in a Community. Based on the reflections and memories of myself and two other psychotherapists, they are vastly different. Each account was written shortly after the placement. They have been edited and identifying details changed to protect the identity of those who were residents. The title of each paper reflects the dominant theme for each therapist. Clearly, each of us found the experience challenging and this was particularly true at the beginning of the placement.

The phantasies of each of us, had not yet been recognised and identified and therefore tested against the reality of community living. And as we discovered, each and every placement evoked different fears. For myself, it was fear of rejection, for Diana, fear of the unknown, for Susan fear of madness, but these were primarily our problems, not theirs. Significantly as time passed, we became aware of our issues in relation to theirs, and we came to understand that in any one narrative the stories ultimately belonged to both.

Since, the role of the trainee psychotherapist working within a Community was never clearly identified, it was up to each of us how we related. In one sense, this was pure happenchance. The overall aim was to understand the thoughts and feelings of the residents before they became problematic. This inevitably was a two-way process. Like the residents, we were already 'in' our own psychotherapy and therefore we assumed we already knew our strengths and weaknesses. We were wrong. This was not the case.

They were curious. They wanted to understand not only themselves but ourselves, and residents had an unerring facility for identifying and then taking aim at our vulnerabilities, our uncertainties, our likes and dislikes. Consequently areas of our own past and our psyches, which had once been hidden or unknown, were brought into the blinding light of the day. For such times we received regular supervision from an experienced Arbours psychotherapist. This gave us a much needed space to think about the psychological problems that group life created. For the trainee this was a necessary and vital part of the Arbours training since it preceded the eventual goal of working analytically on a one-to-one basis. The early experiences were, we eventually discovered, more to do with how, in our work with others on a daily basis, some relationships become repeated. Somehow we would find in each other, as well as ourselves, a kind of familiarity so each side would initially enact their part with very little conscious knowledge or understanding of what or why a particular role was repeated. What is clear, however, is that in each case, the therapist engaged with the residents in a truly authentic search to find some way of resolving and understanding their psychological issues.

— CHAPTER 13 —

Marguerite on 'Favouritism'

Based on an often unspoken hierarchy within a group, favouritism by its nature is corrosive. Maybe it was first experienced in one's family of origin, hence the origins of its power but it is likely to be present in all social groups. Favouritism is based on the belief that someone is preferred because they are seen to be prettier, nicer, or cleverer than others. Many other characteristics can also apply. The outcome of this is the subtle or not so subtle exclusion of another, and further consequences are the accompanying painful feelings of inferiority, hurt, rejection, envy, jealousy and rage. Often the phenomenon is not obvious, which makes it more difficult to challenge. It was a category that during my placement, was to become familiar during my work in the community.

I had first met the residents at their evening meal. With some trepidation I had made my way to the house and rang the bell. I was greeted at the door by Simon, a pale, sickly-looking man. He seemed friendly enough. From there I was taken into the kitchen and offered a cup of tea. Amy sat cutting vegetables up into very small pieces. The eye contact was brief but intense, as if she couldn't maintain a mutual gaze for long. I took a closer look at Simon. He looked like a depressed hippy, and though apparently warm, open and friendly, only his body posture betrayed his troubles. He sat hunched and bent, a concave huddle of distress. Nigel sat smiling broadly. Exuding physical energy, he said he couldn't be there long. He had a game of tennis to play. I later came to understand that this was his way of managing his psychic restlessness and distress.

From there I was taken into the garden. It was a summer's day and I was told that two other members of the community, Fran and Jo, although absent, were looking forward to meeting me. They were concerned they would be late but appeared shortly before the meal. Full of life and colour, Jo with her flaming coloured hair, Fran with a mass of blond hair and very brown, they seemed to fill the room with vivacity and laughter.

Looking back, I was able to see at that very first meeting, each resident had shown an important part of themselves to me and their relationship with each other. What I didn't know was how personally I would experience them, and the intensity of the experience and the 'role.' I was to be allocated. The evening meal passed by without any apparent problem. The whole experience having passed into the mists of time, with the exception of one incident.

While sitting around the kitchen table making fairly polite conversation, the back door opened and a man entered the kitchen. This was Amy's father and without apparently looking at him or greeting him, she said in a fairly cursory manner, 'You're early. We're still eating. Wait for me in my room.'

He made no comment other than as he passed by the table, he said, 'I'm sorry to disturb you.' There was a long silence. Was this apparently off-hand comment significant? I think so. Hardly had he left the room, when Simon was heard to say. 'Doesn't matter ... we're already disturbed.'

His response could be taken straight, or as a wry but humorous observation. I'd got it, but had the others? And if so, how would they respond?

I waited somewhat apprehensively. Suddenly gales of laughter broke out, which I joined. It was a crucial moment. I was new to them and it was a risk but I was accepted. For the next six months I shared their lives with them.

The kitchen was a favourite meeting place for three of the residents, all women, all in their twenties and all having experienced seriously inappropriate parenting. Here they shared thoughts and complaints about themselves and others, while making endless cups of coffee and tea. The kitchen is large, painted white, actually two rooms knocked into one, with a pine table big enough for six people to sit around to share meals. A door leads out into the small, enclosed garden. There is nothing particularly beautiful about the interior of this house, but it's a home offering stability and security to the residents who live there.

Amy, who has a history of self-harm and depression, sits alone at the kitchen table twanging a piece of elastic between her fingers. She looks up as I enter the kitchen. She says, 'I'm bored. I want to go out. Will you come out with me?'

I say, 'Yeah, okay, but where? Where d'you want to go?'

'Ally Pally, the park, it's not far.'

'Fine' (it doesn't occur to me to ask about the two others, Jo and Fran. I assume they're in their rooms either together, or already out, leaving Amy alone). As we walk, Amy tells me how she is constantly left out by Jo and Fran.

'They're like twins,' she says, 'joined at the hip. When they go out, they rarely ask me. They sit together in their rooms. I can hear them laughing. It's as if I don't exist. They totally ignore me.' Her eyes are downcast, her voice flat with no expression.

'Have you spoken to them about this?'

'What's the point?'

'Maybe they're not aware how you feel'

'There's no point talking. They don't care about me.' There was a long silence. She repeats, 'They just don't care. I've told my therapist about them.'

'And what does she say?'

'Same as you ... I'm thinking of leaving. I'm fed up.'

I stop and say, 'Amy, look I know you haven't been in the Community long. Why don't you bring this up at a house meeting? Isn't that the place for problems? Will you do that?'

She shrugs. I say, 'You must ...' She stares silently at me, her eyes filling with tears.

'Come', I say, 'Let's go and look for some decent coffee. I'll get you an almond croissant, I think you'll like them.'

She withdraws from any meaningful conversation, her head bowed, she disappears into her own thoughts. We make our way silently through the trees and towards the road. For the time being, I've decided to wait for her to talk. As we reach the car park, we see the solitary figure of Jo. She is standing alone, her bike propped beside her. She is dressed in her motorbike outfit, looking distraught, and holding her crash helmet in her hands. As she sees us, her face crumples and oblivious to passers-by she begins to cry.

She makes no effort to hide her tears and I feel taken aback with this very public display of distress, I say, 'Jo, let's go somewhere less crowded to talk in private.'

Amy remains silent and apparently unmoved. We sit on a park bench. I sit in the middle.

I say, 'What's wrong? Why are you so upset?' There's a short silence, before she speaks. 'You've only just started. You don't know what's going on ...' She turns her head so she's looking at me directly. I'm aware I'm under intense scrutiny. She's looking resentful and hurt. 'Well, tell me. I want to know.'

'As soon as you came, I knew what would happen. The games. Amy always plays. I said to Fran, she'll try to turn you against us, both of us, me and Fran ... so you'll exclude us and you won't like us ... I was right. You just went out with Amy. You didn't tell us where you were going and you left me and Fran on our own.'

'But I left a note saying we'd gone to the park.'

'Yes, but I wanted you to wait for us, not go out alone with Amy.'

At which point, Amy spoke. 'You're jealous. You and Fran.

You always want to be the student's favourite. You leave me out of everything you do.'

I hardly know them, but I feel shocked by the intensity and how they see each other and myself in relationship to them as a group and as individuals. I say, 'I don't know how to respond.' And 'I don't want to make anyone a favourite … You'll all be special and different to me, once I know you …' Neither speaks. In desperation, I say 'Look, what about one of you bringing this up in the House meeting.' Neither answers.

On return to the Community I'm feeling unsure, and we all behave as if there is no problem. I wait for the House meeting but that comes and goes and no one speaks and I too choose to be silent. I've only just started my placement and I'm way out of my depth. This was my first experience of the intense relationships played out in the Community but as I was about to discover, favouritism and who was seen to have the most attention was to become a constant issue.

Some days later I observe the theme was repeated. Again, it involved all three women and myself. This time I tried to play my role differently. All four of us are sitting round the table in the kitchen.

Fran is painting. She says she'd like to go out for a walk but not right now. She asks if we'll wait for her while she finishes her picture.

I consult Amy and Jo. 'What would you like to do?'

Jo says she's going to be busy but she's happy to wait for Fran, at which point Fran interrupts and says on second thoughts she says she would prefer to go for a swim. She asks if I would like to swim.

I say that I'm not sure what I want to do.

I silently observe Amy is not asked.

I turn to Amy and ask her what she would like to do. Amy says she would like to go but she can't swim because she has a period.

Jo says, 'That's a shame, because I'd like to swim. That's what I want to do.' The comment effectively excludes Amy.

Amy says sarcastically, 'It's not a shame. It suits you. That's your preference. Anything to be alone with her.' She gestures with her thumb toward me.

No one is looking at me. I stare at them. I have no idea what to say. Again, I feel tied in knots. Each has stated a preference which in one way or another, excludes someone else, but at the same time puts me central stage. I am apprehensive. I need to get it right, say the right thing. There's a long silence. Amy picks up her elastic band and begins pinging it. Fran continues painting. Jo puts water in the kettle.

I watch with interest to see how many mugs she puts out. She puts two … who are the chosen two, I wonder. Is it for herself and Fran, Amy and myself, or any other combination? I decide not to ask. I sit down and as the kettle boils, I stand up and put two more mugs out, and ask what they would each like. I decide to cut through the hostile silence.

I say, 'You know it seems really difficult this morning to come to a decision, so let's stay here and not go out. But at some point, we must talk about this in the house meeting, don't you think?' Silence. I search for a distraction. I continue, 'In the meantime, I want to know, if you would like to tell me, about dance therapy because I really have no idea what you do. Do you like it? Do the men dance?'

There's another silence until suddenly Jo looks up and laughs. 'Really, would you really like to know?' I smile and nod. 'You should come because the way Simon dances … well, he's like a ferret trying to escape from a trap. This is him … watch me …' She wiggles her body pointing her hands towards the ceiling. 'You mean like this?' I copy her and laugh as do Fran and Amy.

My intervention had worked, for the moment. Within this short space of time, the competition between the residents and their need to be special to me was now glaringly apparent. How can these relationships be understood?

I take it to supervision and after talking with Tom, I feel clearer. But negotiating a way through these dynamics was not going to be easy, and as I eventually discovered, with time, the relationship between the four of us became even more difficult. Tom takes all my observations calmly.

He says the more the emotional enmeshment between student and resident, the greater the potential for learning. Groups, he says, for us all, express the hopes and fears of early experiences of family life and later reappear. In the case of Fran, Jo and Amy, each of them would have liked my sole attention, to understand them, to make sense of their confusion, to contain their distress, to tolerate their moods. Working within this particular Community, was more demanding for female students.

Fran and Jo in particular, had both experienced within their family of origin an abusive relationship with men and now expressed an open hostility to them. What they sought was an idealised and protective mother, but all three were now involved in a rivalrous and competitive struggle for my attention.

As time passed, the intensity and rivalry between the residents increased. It was not helped by a favourable comparison made by the residents between a past student and myself, which although positive had the effect of making me feel under constant scrutiny. Ultimately, it was controlling. I felt I had to be on my best behaviour. The arrival of a new student, Alice, complicated matters even more. She was to take my place once I left. The enmeshment and competition intensified day by day to the extent I felt I was picking my way through a psychic mine field. One unguarded comment could, I felt, result in disaster.

Meanwhile Fran gave me her version of events. I knew already of the close emotional bond between Fran and Jo. It was glaringly obvious. They were like conjoined twins, speaking out for each other, and a constant source of support for each other.

However, it had not always been so. Fran told me, that prior to my arrival, Jo had become close to Susan, the previous student. This meant Fran had felt left out but the information was useful. Knowing this, I now understood why Fran was gradually making me 'special'. It made sense, because it was a way of getting back at Jo. Whether this was conscious or not, remained unknown and I chose to keep my interpretation to myself.

I did very much like Fran but there were times when I found her interest in me more than annoying. There was often a stream of comments and questions about what I was wearing, where I had been, and what I might have said in supervision. Sometimes she would speak in a baby voice and ask if I would be her mummy.

The whole issue of mothers and daughters was to become a constant theme in the house. The women were constantly on the lookout for who was parenting whom, since if someone else was getting 'mothered', then they were missing out, as it meant they weren't. They also phantasised about what it might be like to be the children of Tom and Sally, the supervising couple for the Community, and what kind of parent they themselves might be. Generally good it seemed, as they would give the baby what they would have liked, but hadn't experienced themselves from their own parents.

This particular issue became 'acted out'[15] as on one particular day I found myself drawn into behaving in the role of a good mother. It was late evening and the three of us, Fran, Jo and myself had spent the afternoon together and now were watching television. It had been a pleasant day, and conflict free, when I told them it was about time for me to leave. This was a regular routine, and not a surprise.

Jo looked dismayed, 'Oh' she said, 'don't go.'

Fran said, You can't go. We want you to stay.'

I said, 'You know I always go at this time.'

There was a heavy silence as the two fixed me with a look that expressed disappointment, regret and sadness. 'I have to go', I said. I stood up.

Fran said, 'Well, will you read to us, before you go.'

'Read to you?'

'Yes'

I felt perplexed. 'What would you like me to read?'

Then I suddenly understood. They were feeling abandoned and reading to them would take away just a little of their feelings of loss. What could be wrong with that? Surely that would be therapeutic.

Fran said she'd find a book and she disappeared, returning a few minutes later with a book of fairy tales. 'You choose' she said.

---

15 'Acting out' is a technical term and refers to when an action is repeated and not verbalised, thereby losing its emotional significance.

I sat down and read 'Sleeping Beauty' aware that the point of this story was the rescue of a beautiful woman by a handsome prince. I guessed that at some level this reflected an unspoken wish to also be rescued from their own unhappiness.

But at some level, the incident didn't seem right and later after talking through this incident with Tom, he confirmed my apprehension. He pointed out that despite my desire to behave sensitively and therapeutically to mitigate their disappointment at my leaving, in actual fact I had, unwittingly, confirmed their dependency and disappointment. By reading to them, I had related to them as if they were small children. I was reminded that they were young women with a history of emotional dependency, with feelings of low self-esteem and inadequacy. Part of the work was to gradually help them understand and overcome this which had been so debilitating to them. I found this insight really helpful, probably because it took away some pressure I felt to keep them happy.

When it came to the actual time for me to leave the Community, there was a fresh crisis. It was already known that when a student left, it was always a difficult time for the residents as it invariably aroused ambivalence, sadness and depressive feelings. But my leaving also coincided with other changes. Nigel who had been a long standing and important member of the community moved out, and Jo who had already developed a close relationship with Alice, the new visiting student, who would replace me after I had left, had fallen out with her.

I felt I was in the middle of a seething cauldron with very little time to think. The consequence was a major split between myself and Alice. It happened like this; I was sitting alone in the kitchen waiting for Alice to arrive. She was fifteen minutes late which meant I couldn't go until she arrived and that annoyed me.

Alice says, 'I'm sorry I'm late. I got held up by the traffic.'

Me, 'But you're always late, and I had said, I needed to be away on time'.

'I've told you, I'm sorry, what more can I do?'

'What about making sure, just for once, that you arrive on time?'

'What's your problem, are you never late?'

'Now and again, but if someone asks me especially to be on time, then I'm on time.'

'Well good for you.' She turns away to put the kettle on, and then without looking at me, says, 'Has anyone ever told you how difficult you are?'

I said, 'That's funny, I was thinking the same about you, and right now, I feel under some kind of attack from you.'

'You're always needling me.'

'It's in your head.'

'It was obvious from the start you didn't like me'

'Really? ... You need to talk about that to your therapist. I'm going. Have a good evening,' I stood up to leave, just as Fran entered. She immediately picked up on the bad atmosphere.

'What's going on?'

Alice didn't answer. I shrug my shoulders and said 'Just a minor dispute. Must go. I'm late.'

At this point Alice decides to speak. She says, 'Oh, "minor", that's what she says, but it's my fault ... like it always is.'

Following this exchange, the bad vibes between us became very obvious and this unsettled every resident. Alice became the recipient of all the negative feelings within the Community, including those from myself. I now noticed she was never there when I was there. It felt as if she was avoiding me. The house meetings, the place where all the residents and the students met to discuss difficult issues, which was usually a safe place, became heavy with long and angry silences. Meanwhile the closer the time to my leaving came, the more difficult it was to understand and contain what seemed an increasingly crazy atmosphere.

One afternoon all five of the residents and myself were sitting round the kitchen table. This had never happened before. I was asked whether I'd miss them when I left, and whether I would cry. The laughter was manic, loud and unrestrained, and I felt under enormous pressure to behave in a similar way. There was still considerable anger with Alice and the fact she had been invited, on our joint supervisor's advice, to my leaving meal, only escalated the negative feelings towards her. All the hostility and hate was now focused on her, whereas I was seen as the warm, understanding student. I dreaded the leaving meal fearing a blow up between Alice and myself.

However when the time came, despite all these incidents, and the splitting between 'the good and the bad', the leaving meal was enjoyable. Or so it seemed. Outwardly, the residents were polite to Alice but after she briefly left the house to buy more wine, the blame and hostility re-emerged, only to be pushed away and hidden in the false expressions of interest as she again took her place at the table. All the negative feelings remained but temporarily were hidden under the veneer of civilised conversation. I, however was grateful for this restraint. I felt I was walking a tightrope and if I said the wrong thing or did something that could be seen as provocative, I would fall off or be pushed into the flames of hell that lay in wait.

Leaving the Community left me with feelings of deep sadness. I had become involved with each one of them, but in different ways. I knew also I represented to them various people from the past; mothers, sisters, friends, lovers. I had enormous admiration for their ongoing attempts to escape from the past, for their honesty, and for their often painful struggles to engage in relationships with each other. The gift to which they all contributed, was deeply personal. Each had painted on a horizontal scroll their thoughts and feelings about my time there. I knew I would miss them. Somehow, they had entered my soul.

I told them of a poem by Sheenagh Pugh. It was a favourite of mine and called 'Sometimes' it addresses the disappointments and sadness of the past with the hopes of the future.[16] In another poem Elma Mitchell observes the power of words and poetry such as this saying, 'Words/Can seriously affect your heart'.[17]

---

16 See https://pwrites.princeton.edu/poem/a-poem-for-you-sometimes-by-sheenagh-pugh
17 See https://mybeautfulthings.com/tag/elma-mitchell

Robert Hinshelwood, a psychiatrist and also a group therapist, wrote, 'The community accepts despairing people. The impact on the "staff" of people who {have} put their last hopes in the hands of the staff is taxing. The acute sensitivity of the patients to the condition of the staff to whom they have turned to so desperately, reacts with the staff's sensitivity to being placed in the position of the last hope.'

Being a trainee psychotherapist at an Arbours Community gave me the opportunity of experiencing this in a profoundly moving way and I knew then as I know now, that this could never be repeated. I felt privileged to have experienced this and I shall always value that time.

Postscript 2023

Writing about and reliving those intense times with the residents has re-awakened powerful memories, particularly Tom's comment on how early experiences of groups influence our later behaviour, wishes and fears. Thinking about this years later, I now fully understand that the whole issue of competition and jealousy for my attention then, was a re-run of my first years. My very young mother had left me on a daily basis in the care of my great aunt who was childless. The memory of their fights and squabbles over me as to who was the better mother and who I loved the most, although implicit, has always been a disturbing memory but one I had tried to avoid.

These experiences were unwittingly re-enacted during my stay in the Community. Somehow the problems of my childhood were communicated and worked through with the residents, which to me at least, not only demonstrates the continuing power of the unconscious but also the particular sensitivity towards others of those with disturbed emotional histories.

— CHAPTER 14 —

Diana on 'Knowing and Not Knowing'

It's many years since I did my placement in an Arbours community but something strikes me now, not obvious at the time. This was the residents' awareness of my work. I was a manager in Social Services and looking back this was more significant than I realised, when I think about the relationship between myself and the residents.

From the start they commented on how 'nice' it was to have an older person. This led me to fantasise about what kind of mother I had been, and by implication, what kind of maternal figure I would be to them. Signs of their anxiety about my presence was also shown by how much information they had gathered about me before I arrived. This may be seen as a natural curiosity, but it might also indicate an apprehension about my use of authority towards them. For example, during one of the meals we shared, one of the residents raised this in terms of a query as to my role as a social worker. Their evident apprehension about how I might use my authority might partly be explained by what seemed their hidden anger of my not being in the community over Christmas and the consequent difficulties of organising the shared meal with them. It was perhaps a way of rebelling and of resisting my authority.

At the beginning of my placement, I'd been invited to come to the house for tea but I hadn't a clue what to expect. As a Manager in a Social Services Department, it had occurred to me how my team would smile if they could see me standing on the doorstep without a remit or task to accomplish.

I was ushered into the kitchen by Ruth and Natalie. They were concerned, asking if I had found the house easily and whether I'd had a good drive into London. They commented that it would be nice to have an older person in the Community. This felt a loaded statement and its meaning, as expressed by them both, soon became apparent. I wondered whether they had phantasies of my being a mother figure and reflected how my grown-up children would have enjoyed this, because they never lost an opportunity to remind me how I could have been a better mother.

It quickly became apparent how much the residents knew of me. They knew where I lived, that I was a social worker and as time went on in the placement, I was frequently confronted with their need to know more. This included everything and everybody who was of any significance to me. It felt as if they had to know everything before they felt they knew me, and that they found it impossible to discover a relationship as it unfolded.

Knowing as much as they could was safe, or as safe as it could be; not knowing was uncontained and risky and would lend itself to being the object of phantasy or made up. When pressed they would good-naturedly admit to this.

Ruth and Natalie gave me what they saw as the rundown on the house. Ruth seemed to have taken on the role of head housekeeper or resident therapist, and in passing told me that the last student had been perfect. I made no comment. Susan, the third woman then appeared. Apparently, she'd been asleep upstairs and later but when Ruth and Natalie were busy with domestic tasks, she had leant towards me and rather ominously had said, 'There's a lot of bad feelings in the house, and people have great difficulty with their anger. I hope you can stand it.' I understood this comment to be a warning but also a rejection.

A fourth woman, Valerie appeared, but after briefly saying 'Hello' she announced she was going out. Ruth told me that Valerie had lived there for many years and apparently she always had problems with new students.

Ruth was keen to show me her artwork. I had already noticed the paintings. In fact it was difficult to avoid them. They engulfed the house. Mostly painted by Ruth in the Art Therapy workshop, every room depicted something which to me seemed quite bizarre. For example, at the bottom of the stairs was an enormous painting of a contorted nude woman. Personally, I would have found this difficult to live with, and I later discovered that Susan also felt strongly that this particular painting was distasteful and disrespectful to women.

However, Ruth was keen to know my response. This confronted me with a dilemma. Should I say I found them unsettling and that I did not understand them, or should I say nothing? I eventually chose to say nothing, on the grounds it was probably only myself that found them so disturbing. I have to say I saw the paintings of these women as particularly ugly; their appearance almost abusive, with their bloated, contorted stomachs and strange stances.

But as time went on, I began to understand their significance. This was how Ruth saw her body. It seemed she was unable to speak of her distress, rather it was somatised and expressed through her body. Occasionally, her stomach would become so grossly distended it necessitated several hospital admissions.

However, the longer the time I spent with the residents, the more aware I became of their continuing interest in me as a social worker, and their concern about how this might influence how I related to them. For example, I was sitting one afternoon at the kitchen table talking with Susan and Alan, when Alan had said, 'So you make families nice to each other in your work, do you?' He said this with a smile on his face. I was taken aback with his comment and replied rather lamely, 'I am not sure you can do this.'

On another occasion, Natalie had said, 'I hope you keep children safe and don't let them be abused by their parents and families' to which Susan responded, 'Well, now we have a Resident Social Worker in the house.' I found these comments somewhat unsettling and debated within myself what they might mean.

Natalie had told me of her childhood abuse and that her parents were members of the False Memory Syndrome Group. Her parents refused to believe her allegation of sexual abuse within the family. She seemed frightened of rejecting her family but drawn to them on the occasions when they rang her.

Ruth had already told me of her abusing idealised brothers, and of her own intrusive, controlling mother. She said she was scared of being with her family and needed protection from them. Sometimes, she said, her mother would come to the Community and push her way in, leaving Ruth powerless to ask her to leave. Despite these comments, I had heard her on occasions talking to her mother on the phone in a very animated fashion, as they made arrangements to see her family. As with Natalie, the need for a loving family and their actual childhood experiences were in conflict and any form of resolution at the time seemed impossible to navigate.

Susan spoke of never experiencing any care or love and on one occasion she said something to me that I shall never forget. Perhaps it was the way she told me. Her childhood had been barren, but she said that the worst thing for her was coming to terms with the fact she could not go back and have the love from her parents she had always craved. This was so hard for her, she sometimes wondered if she would or could survive it. As I heard this, I was aware of my own distress for her and that as I responded, my voice quivered.

One evening early in the placement, I developed a terrible headache and although I hadn't normally slept overnight in the house, I asked whether I could stay rather than drive the long way home. Ruth immediately flew out of the room up to the airing cupboard and found me clean bedding. She also insisted I wore one of her clean T-shirts to sleep in. Eventually I ushered her out of the bedroom and began to get ready for bed.

There was a knock on the door. Susan was standing outside. She had bought me a clean pillow cover and towel she had washed that afternoon. She said they smelt nice with softener and that would be pleasant for me. I told her she was very kind and thinking about this afterwards, I realised in their own ways they were looking after me, tucking me up in bed with the kindness and concern they would have liked as children themselves and still wanted.

I slept soundly until early morning when I woke with a start. I had heard a terrible noise like a dog howling, but then with horror, I realised that it was me. My heart sank. I wondered what I would say in the morning. The dream, which was in fact a nightmare, was about my own family dynamics and how I saw myself.

It was apparent that the residents had touched my own inner struggles in a very profound way and this was the content of my own disturbance. I was reminded of a comment made by Nina Coltart. She had written that while the therapist is intimately related to the patient's inner object-world, she must also remain detached. Only thus can she retain her own subjectivity while still remaining for the patient their psychic object.[18]

As well as myself, two other students began their placement at the community. On one particular day Ruth and Natalie were waiting for me when I arrived and they made it clear that they had the afternoon planned. I shall never know to this day how they knew I enjoyed shopping. I was taken down to Wood Green Shopping Centre and they pointed out the banks, the big chain stores and showed me the car parks. They were on a mission to buy clothes for Alan as his birthday present from the house. We must have gone into every clothes shop in Wood Green. Alan was to be the owner of a set of clothes, and I was assured these would do wonders for his image. If I hadn't already met Alan, I would easily have thought he was the school child being bought a uniform in his absence.

---

18 Nina Coltart, in *The Baby And The Bathwater*, Ch. 2, 'Why Am I Here?', p.28. International Universities Press, 1996.

However they were also interested in my thoughts and opinions of the two new students. They expressed concern about one particular student but when I refused to engage with them, I was told I was a hard woman. I suggested they talk directly to the student or bring the issue up at a house meeting.

Apart from this, there were also two vacancies in the house, and whether they were to be filled by men or women residents became a major problem. Ruth and Natalie said they could not cope with more men. Ruth told me they were difficult, and sometimes smelly. Unlike Tom, (the Arbours supervisor) who, she assured me was wonderful in every way. She also said she could not get on with women and only felt relaxed in the company of men which she put down to her relationship with her brothers. In fact, she said she saw herself as an honorary man, but also felt that the presence of a man would prevent her thinking about her sexuality.

I was confused by these apparently contradictory messages, and said if the house was kept as a safe place, she ought to be able to begin to explore her sexuality. I further said personally I enjoyed the company of men. She was not impressed. She gave me a withering look and said, 'If you lived here, you wouldn't want more men in the house.'

At that point, Natalie who had been listening intently to the conversation, stood up and stretched, and said, 'Oh well, I'm going for a shit'. Thus graphically, if crudely, communicated her thoughts and feelings. Not for the first time, I noticed that it was difficult for some residents to keep both positive and negative feelings integrated. People were seen as either one or the other and anything too disturbing was evacuated.

Tom however was adamant that the house did need the presence of men, and two young men by the names of Max and Alex were suggested. Eventually they moved in. Both had backgrounds of living in other therapeutic communities. Max appeared to settle, but soon began complaining that people were talking behind each other's backs. By people, he meant other residents and students. Ruth was outraged, and as a consequence Max took to spending more and more time in his room. He also appeared to believe that others were talking about him in the streets and was clearly becoming more and more distressed.

Alex meanwhile announced in a House Meeting he found Natalie attractive. Valerie and Ruth responded to this by asking, 'What's wrong with us?' as if they thought of themselves as the two ugly sisters. This was to have a profound effect on some of the women.

Ruth for example, later confided in me that she had stapled up her vagina, which I shared this information with Tom in supervision. We understood this as a symbolic statement. Otherwise, it would have been impossible for her to sit cross-legged as she told me about this. I didn't however communicate this back to her, but mentally ran over the route to the nearest Accident and Emergency Department. It seemed as if this was Ruth's way of making a dramatic statement based on her need to close herself up to the presence of men.

Shortly after Alex's admission that he found Natalie attractive, it was noticeable she began losing weight. When pressed, she said she was taking laxatives. She was also seeing a female gynaecologist for exploratory examinations regarding some internal problems which were she said, a result of her past sexual abuse.

Meanwhile, Valerie and Susan began to miss meals. They would separately prepare a snack for themselves but then say they were not hungry and leave the prepared meals on the table. It seemed that when any of them were distressed or angry, they found it difficult to take anything in.

Alongside this, I noticed Alex was avoiding me. I felt sure this was because he disliked me. Nevertheless, when he verbally attacked me in a House Meeting, I was taken by surprise. He was extremely angry. He said I was never there and I should not be considered as part of the house. That night he was admitted to hospital crying, vomiting, and had also lost control of his bowels. No specific cause was found for these symptoms, but by now it was clear I had become the object of his dislike.

His avoidance of me continued. Eventually it reached a stage that after observing and totally ignoring me while he spoke with others, I angrily said I found him annoying and very rude. We spent the next hour talking. He said I was like his sister with whom he had great difficulties.

Christmas presented its own problems. I had planned to cook a meal on Christmas Eve but one by one they told me that for various reasons, it would be impossible to attend at the time allocated. Much time and effort had been spent on the side issue of the Christmas tree and when it would be put up. I had assumed cooking a meal would be straightforward but this was not the case. I continually asked what they would like but nobody could be specific. I was told that there was nothing in particular, but that it shouldn't be either rich or fancy. After repeated requests I put my foot down and said I would choose. I proposed a particular time and said if anyone was late, those of us there would go ahead with or without them.

This worked. The meal seemed to be enjoyed, but I sensed their anger towards me. They were concerned that there was not going to be a student therapist over Christmas and asked me many questions about how I would spend time at home. Although another resident psychotherapist would be contactable, this was not enough, especially for Ruth.

As with the previous Christmas break, she fell off her scooter and hurt her leg. Natalie stated she wanted to change her therapist. Alex told us that he had 'shaved his balls' because they were of no use to him without a woman. He said that when he became distressed he would think about what it must be like to be a woman and put on a dress and paint his nails red. However, on my return, Alan welcomed me with 'Oh, you still love us then, you've come back.'

Two weeks before I was due to leave, a message was put on the House noticeboard stating that a new student would replace me. It laid out in meticulous detail her times to the extent it was glaringly obvious they were critical of how much little time I had spent with them. I knew I always handled goodbyes badly and would avoid them, if possible.

In one of my final House Meetings, Tom had asked how the placement had affected me. I mumbled and fumbled for the words. I said it had put me in touch with my vulnerability and that I often took a deep breath as I put the key in the door. Susan was very surprised by this. They had observed that I sang when I was anxious and would complain about the top of the oven being dirty. But I also knew that being in the Community had been very important to me. There had been good times, plenty of times when we shared laughter, but other times when I experienced irritation and naked anger as I left.

When it came to leaving, I had not expected the painting Valerie gave me. All the residents had contributed to it and I was taken by surprise but very touched. Ruth then showed me who had painted what and as she did so, I commented on each part: the picture of a little, old man with round glasses was painted by Max. The man had a little, white dog on a lead and stood in the middle of a field. There was a large rainbow in the background and a menacing dark mountain under the sun, while in one corner of the picture was a large sunflower. It made me wonder whether he would ever reach such a settled life, but I hoped he would.

Alan had painted the rainbow. He had often told me there was nothing for him in life, it was all a con. I said I hoped he'd find what he wanted at the end of the rainbow. Natalie had painted the large sunflower at the front of the picture. The flower was strong and fully opened. I wished that for Natalie.

Ruth had painted a large sunhat but also rain and I hoped she would learn to cope with both.

Valerie had painted the dark mountain and I hoped she would eventually climb hers.

Alex had painted the cloud and the birds. I also hoped he managed to survive the clouds but soar with the freedom of the birds.

I thanked the Community for teaching me how to say goodbye. Eventually I said I had to go. All the residents with the exception of Valerie gave me a spontaneous hug. The spontaneity touched me. I had not always seen eye to eye with the residents, but I think we acknowledged we were all in the struggle together and we could survive falling out and having different opinions. I felt privileged to have spent time with them.

— CHAPTER 15 —

Susan on 'The Mad Tea Party'

> *'But I don't want to go among mad people',*
> *Alice remarked.*
> *'Oh you can't help that said the cat:*
> *We're all mad here. I'm mad. You're mad.'*
> *'How do you know I'm mad?' said Alice.*
> *'You must be,' said the cat,*
> *'or you wouldn't have come here'.*

Why did I choose *Alice in Wonderland* as a metaphor for my experience and review of my time at the Arbours Community? Children's fantasies evoke powerful truths about the most primitive parts of ourselves and in their terrifying immediacy, the boundaries between fantasy and sanity are often not clearly defined. Alice's adventures are shifting and forever unpredictable, mixing dream with nightmare and fantasy with reality. It's a world where a Cheshire cat disappears and reappears in a 'fort da' game confronting Alice with her deepest anxieties. She asks the cat 'Could you tell me, please, which way I ought to go from here?' to which the cat replies, 'That depends a good deal on where you want to get to.' There are no answers. She has to find her own way.

Likewise in the community, there were few maps or signposts to point the way. Initially, I was given an interview whereby the residents of the Community had agreed to accept me. I was aware of my vulnerability. Here were people who had far more therapy than me, interrogating me and wanting to know what felt like 'too much.' Like Alice in Wonderland, grabbing at straws, wanting her books and the familiar, I scanned my mind for theories that would make sense to help me cope with these feelings.

That first night, I had dreams of being assaulted by the residents and longed to be back with my mother. The dream made some sense. I feared leaving behind my 'mother tongue' and I was anxious about the unknown awaiting me. Similar dreams followed, all relating to madness, and the torn loyalties between family and the community at Arbours.

Alice had spoken of feeling caught between two worlds; a longing to explore the wonder and terror but also the longing to return to safety and familiarity. She was lost in a dream of strange creatures and struggled with losing her identity. From discovering the jar of 'Drink Me' to arriving at the jar of 'Understand Me' was a process. Alice waited, to see if she was going to shrink further. She felt a little nervous about this, 'for it might end, you know, in my going out altogether like a candle'.

Prior to starting at the Community, I had had a dream: where a crowd of mad people invaded me. Like caricatures from *One Flew Over the Cuckoo's Nest* they had intense looks of anguish on their faces resembling Picasso's painting 'Guernica.' They were making impossible demands, and feeling so exasperated, I ran into my room for shelter. One of the residents followed me and I could not tell them to leave. My 'rite de passage' was about to begin.

'The rabbit-hole went straight on like a tunnel for some way, and then dipped suddenly down, so suddenly that Alice had not a moment to think about stopping herself before she found herself falling down a very deep well.'

My first day in the community. I felt immediately sucked into a deep well of nameless dread. I felt the strong desire to escape. I was greeted by Derek, a young man I had met at the interview, who seemed to trigger some of my disturbing dreams. I felt nervous around him, not knowing whether this feeling came from me or him. He was dressed as if he was a Goth. He drew from his pocket a picture of a formidable looking Jesus with black blood dripping down his forehead, and said to me that 'Jesus was the son of the devil'. He wanted to interview me and record the conversation. Feeling too confused to disagree, I acquiesced.

When he asked about my religion, I refused to answer and attempting to find some common ground, I pointed out that all religions believed in respect and love for everyone, whatever the individual differences. I said we should do unto others what we would expect for ourselves. At this, he laughed hysterically, dangling a large screw in front of me as he sipped coffee. Then suddenly he jumped up to leave but looking at his coffee, he said, 'Someone might put something in it. I better take it'. I dared him to leave the coffee, which he did. I was aware that he needed to try to control me but by now I felt that we had a common language in humour.

Derek's favourite pastime was watching violent films which we did together, at times in virtual silence. I felt he wanted desperately for someone to break through and make contact, but that he could not break free from the sinister world he was trapped in. He said he appreciated that I was less afraid of him. He occasionally would talk about feelings of emptiness.

Everyone in the house was preoccupied with Derek. He made sadistic remarks at meetings, and later on, when the coordinators were on holiday, he became involved in physical fights with another resident. Two women with a history of being abused sexually were particularly frightened by Derek's interest in pornography, which he watched in addition to the horror films. These seemed to stir up powerful sexual and aggressive feelings they kept locked away.

The Community held regular house meetings where the facilitator explored what feelings had been stirred up arising from events and others' actions. This seemed safe. Focusing on other issues, particularly when talking about residents who were leaving, helped to cover up my own difficulty with arriving. I wanted to be the seasoned student who already knew all the ropes. I had an image of a roll of film that needed exposing image by image but also wishing it was already at the last frame.

After the first house meeting, I found it difficult to abandon these troubled people and felt compelled to stay late during the first few weeks. The weight of feelings in the house was so strong and disorienting that it took time to adjust and shake off the guilt about leaving them to fend for themselves.

At the Mad Tea Party, the Mad Hatter and Time have an argument. Time refuses to allow the tea party to end. Time is frozen and the idea of real time passing is non-existent. For me in the Community, it often felt like being in a time warp, suspended in space without time and like Alice's Tea Party, the only movement occurring was in the rotation around the table.

People were often caught up in repetitive, self-absorbing patterns which seemed to go nowhere and as if there was no world outside. Dirty dishes would accumulate and there was no real food. This was particularly noticeable when the Coordinators went away for 10 days. This also meant there was no therapy during that time. There was a lot of tension and I wondered how I would cope. When faced with uncertainty, I would try to maintain a sense of familiarity by sipping endless cups of tea, and like Alice, I felt comforted by food. I was both concerned and reassured by the prospect of being seen as a servant or mother figure. I realised that responding to the role of mother felt safer than experiencing their turmoil as well as my own.

With Tom and Sally away, the residents felt unsafe and abandoned as if the coordinators were 'bad parents.' Fantasies of an abandoning and depriving mother were projected and relationships in the house were fraught with anxiety. At such times they longed for me to become an idealised mother to fulfil their needs. Derek's aggression became more unbearable as they felt the need for 'more protection and weekend cover'. The residents thought that Arbours should be dealing with this problem and we should get rid of Derek before Tom and Sally got back.

Residents were beginning to let me in on their early childhood experiences of abuse and abandonment. Luke told me about his early life. Abandoned by his mother at three months, the neighbours heard a baby crying endlessly and he was rescued, only to be physically abused later by his adoptive mother. He also said he had been sexually abused by various men as a young child. Luke had two other adopted brothers by whom he felt pushed out and found it hard to trust anyone. He was thinking of leaving so he could belong somewhere. Allowing himself space in the house was painful. His fight with Derek had reawakened feelings of violence and the powerful need to leave.

When Rachel, another resident, came in the room Luke left abruptly in a huff. Rachel found it difficult to share me with anyone and would get into the middle whenever I was with another student or resident. She would quickly fill the room with her own agenda, protesting: 'you are exactly like my mother. I used to have to wait forever as a child until she returned from the local pub.' She spoke about her experience of violence and abuse, and suffered with debilitating anxiety. She found it unbearable to be alone and mostly was in the house when I was there.

To Amanda, I symbolised the good mother she never had but also the irresponsible mother who could not protect her from abuse. On one visit, Amanda had become alarmed when I told her I was leaving my daughter with her father during my weekend away. She told me her own father had abused her as a very young child; and her mother had not protected her. Often she would become intrusive to the point at which I began to feel immense anger and hate toward her. She would reproach me: 'you probably go to the hairdresser every week and drive a posh car ... I bet you have a five bedroom house with a pool, just like my mum, she was glam and had money too.' At the same time, I felt she wanted to get close but didn't know how. I felt sad and imagined what it must have been like for her to have no private place of her own.

Amanda's world was plagued with secrets she was forced to withhold as a child and she had no sense of privacy. She would share private things which she forbade me to share with others. This became uncomfortable and tormenting. As the weeks passed, I was less intimidated by her projections and helped her to make sense of them in a nonintrusive way. It was helpful to her that I was not devastated by her intrusive love nor her intrusive behaviour. Learning to maintain my own boundaries while still allowing her in, I began to feel less invaded.

While I was still a visiting student, Amanda and Derek had a sexual relationship. Derek however was incapable of relating on an intimate level. Unsupported by the other residents, she stopped eating and spoke of suicide, having become enraged that we were not protecting her. Finally, with my encouragement, she raised this at the next house meeting. This was an important step as she gradually felt safer. When Derek was asked to leave the house, she stayed and continued her relationship with him outside the house, at first very disturbed by his departure.

My need to bring out the good in people eventually became too much because soon the residents were fearful of expressing their nasty side. I gradually withdrew from this role, realising that my way of defending against discomfort was to become involved in dyadic relationships. This also reflected the fragmentation in the Community; we were either islands unto ourselves or able to relate only on a one-on-one basis.

Alice is always ahead of herself and tries to open doors too soon. The curiosity behind the urgency to open doors and the frustration when this was not possible, was strongly felt in the beginning. I needed to wait until people allowed me in. There were doors that did not open. I learned to accept that some people could not allow me into their space. I discovered that needing to resolve issues quickly was not helpful and staying with feelings and conflict, my own and theirs, could result in shifts and create meaning.

When my weekend live-in time began officially, I initially felt lost and uneasy. I was no longer an important guest nor an unwanted visitor. In the house, I shook off the labels of good or bad mother. Becoming a weekend student was an important turning point as people came to experience my darker side. I became more real to them. They became more comfortable with their anger and I wasn't so fearful of my own. I came to trust in my ability to restore myself and was not as afraid when I felt more fragmented.

I was often faced with rude and hostile remarks and would respond politely, particularly after leaving them for the weekend or after a holiday. When I returned, I gave them each a small jar of maple syrup. They responded with indifference or snarky remarks and Vivienne, who will be described later, cooked a beef casserole in spite of my making it clear from the beginning of my stay that I didn't eat meat. I told her sarcastically that she had made a nice welcoming meal in honour of my return. Out of all the people in the house, I found Vivienne the most difficult. She denied that cooking meat was a personal attack.

But in a later house meeting, she said she felt like a 'terrible human being', and deserved to be thrown out, which the residents did not accept. To Vivienne I seemed to represent parts of her world she desperately tried to disown, particularly her sense of identity and her vulnerability. After this meeting, I felt sad for her but also anger.

Becoming a live-in weekend student had stirred up much anxiety about leaving my family. The residents were understanding about my anxieties. They put up a Welcome sign in the hall and a large bowl of fresh fruit meant for me. Luke cleaned the kitchen. There was an electric blanket on my bed and fresh flowers on the bedside table in my room. Vivienne originally said she couldn't make it to dinner but appeared for a short while.

Both Rachel and Amanda asked if they could come to my house for tea. I said they would need to wait until the end of my stay to see how I felt about keeping in touch. Rachel, speaking for Amanda as well said, 'We can be a bit much. I bet we are worse than your children sometimes. But we also wanted to test your boundaries.'

"'If you knew Time as well as I do" said the Hatter, "you wouldn't talk about wasting it". "I don't know what you mean said Alice". "Of course, you don't the Hatter said, tossing his head contemptuously. "I dare say you never even spoke to Time!" "Perhaps not." Alice cautiously replied "but I know I have to beat time when I learn music.'"

Alice's fairly structured life becomes fragmented and her dream becomes a nightmarish awakening. Throughout the story, her thoughts seem filled with unconscious morbidity. Everywhere there is an absurd notion of death as represented by the foreboding doors; the muse; the mock turtle's sad tale and the Queen of Hearts is the Goddess of Death herself. Alice thinks she knows time because she beats it but beating time is as mad as denying the passage of time. Alice begins to look at her own madness instead of setting herself apart from the rest of the creatures.

In the house, people seemed to be in denial of external reality for a good part of the time, as if living in a fantasy that life would go on forever and Arbours would look after them. After all, a few had been living there for almost a decade. The shortness of life and the reality of death were not something they could face. Equally, I became aware of beating time by always wanting to be ahead of myself and needing to be in control. Towards the end of my stay, my own rude awakening put me in touch with mortality and the fragility of life.

My ex-husband had a heart attack at the wheel and suddenly died at 45, leaving my 17-year old daughter without a father. This experience brought me face to face with the finality in the passage of time that awaits all of us. Life was chaotic at home but I returned to Church Lane after a couple of weeks, finding everyone concerned about me. I was no longer split between home and the Church Lane house but I found it difficult this time to be attentive to everyone's needs.

Vivienne and Rachel offered their support. Rachel told me she knew I felt like a mess inside but also knew there was something solid about me. She said that it was important for them to see that one can experience a lot of pain and still hold on. I felt her genuineness; these moments were appreciated, although infrequent. I also knew I would be leaving soon. Rachel was having dreams about separating from her mother and wanted me to leave her my candlesticks so she could think of me when she goes to sleep. Amanda wanted to stay in touch which I agreed to do.

The final weekend arrived and I felt sad. We had shared good and bad times, love and hate and even fun. Although I was an integral part of the community, I knew my life was elsewhere. Amanda cooked the evening meal. There was a beautiful candlelit meal of fresh salmon, gourmet vegetables with chilled wine and a background of jazz music.

I was presented with a hand painted chest that became a mirror when opened. Everyone had worked on this project except Luke. Rachel said the gift symbolised part of what I meant for them: a container for their feelings and a mirror that reflected them. Amanda painted the border, Vivienne and Paul airbrushed the lid and Allen put a black velvet lining into the base, symbolising his dark core (as he later explained). Rachel, still needing centre stage, painted the mirror-frame and card. Mirrors were significant to her, she said, because she wore her Barbie watch with a mirror to therapy so she could see her, without the therapist realising this. We all laughed. Vivienne didn't come but I understood endings were difficult for her. I was moved to tears. The following morning was solemn.

Conclusion

I did not go mad with the residents but I did attempt to enter their world. Only when I began to experience myself in relation to others, understanding their projections and my own, could I begin to make sense of what was happening to me. In Wonderland, Alice is sucked into fantasies and desperately tries to hold on to her capacity to think rationally, to hold onto herself. She learns that, to survive, she needs to hold the paradox of believing and not believing, as I often had to do there. She, as I did, eventually accepts the paradoxes in Wonderland, suspending her beliefs as a way into the world of the other, where, from a safe distance, she could explore her own contradictions and sense of unreality.

R.D. Laing writes in *The Divided Self*, 'the therapist must have the plasticity to transpose himself into another strange and even alien view of the world. In this act, he draws on his own psychotic possibilities without foregoing his sanity. Only thus can he arrive at an understanding of the patient's *existential position*.'[19] Upon reading Laing's *Politics of Experience*, I came to view the people in Church Lane as troubled and distressed rather than as alien and mad, and to quote Laing, more like 'bemused and crazed creature" in many ways, like myself and all of us, 'strangers to our true selves',[20] 'divided selves'.

In Lewis Carroll's story, Alice too experiences the madness of Wonderland without losing her sanity. Her initial reaction is one of extreme loneliness and she feels even more lost when attempting to understand that world using academic knowledge, thus setting herself apart from the creatures. This reflected a divided desperate self that can only transform when Alice learns to use her flexibility to relate in a shared reality with others.

For me experiencing feelings of isolation at first was very painful. I too sought comfort in theories, counting on them to make the pain comprehensible and tolerable. I eventually came to understand that this abstract approach was insufficient. In Wonderland, each of the characters seem to be disowned aspects of Alice's internal world that she eventually reclaims. The Mouse and the Mock Turtle represent her sadness, the White Rabbit her anxiousness, the Queen of Hearts her anger. At Church Lane, I began pushing away the darker aspects of the residents which I came to understand also as difficult aspects of myself: like Rachel's greed, Luke's anger, Vivienne's depression and Derek's deadness.

---

19   R. D. Laing, *The Divided Self: An Existential Study in Sanity and Madness*, p. 34. Pelican, 1964.
20   R. D. Laing, *The Politics of Experience and The Bird of Paradise*, p. 12. Penguin, 1967.

The therapeutic community can be seen as a transitional space between inner and outer reality where one is willing to hold on to uncertainties without reaching finite truths. It is an experience which unfolds in a shared space with others.

Thinking and Feeling

'Winnicott described trauma at the beginning of life, relating it to the threat of annihilation; going to pieces, falling forever, having no relation to the body, having no orientation, complete isolation. The psychoses were to him an environmental defence against the trauma of unthinkable anxieties. Working in the Crisis Centre, we came to see and to recognise such states of mind. Anxieties: of loss, of dreams, of absences, of panic, of meaninglessness, of landscapes bereft of sound, of people struck dumb, terrorised by a life lived without meaning or love.'

— CHAPTER 16 —

How can 'Mental Illness' be Understood?

By using the term 'mentally ill' I'm referring to those who have been medically diagnosed with, for example, clinical depression, bi-polar, or schizophrenia, but also I'm including in this category those who remain free of a diagnosis but seek therapeutic help for feeling troubled, anxious, or depressed. I include these potential patients because it is not uncommon that they refer to themselves as 'mentally ill' and along with that 'self-diagnosis' comes the inevitable fear of being, or going 'mad'.

'Mental illness' as used by the medical profession and some other professionals has a much tighter meaning than the broad category above. It usually implies a belief in the 'medical model' which while acknowledging the possibility of an environmental aspect to a mental illness, the emphasis is on the biological as a primary cause. Consequently, patients categorised in this way are treated with various types of psychotropic medication which affect mood, perception and energy levels. And these, in the long term can cause neurological problems as well as causing weight gain, anxiety, and blurred vision. Patients with more severe symptoms where there is a danger of serious harm to themselves and others, may be subject to a 'section' i.e. incarceration under the terms of the Mental Health Act.

In terms of therapeutic practice, many therapists make no distinction between such patients. They choose not to divide their patients into the 'mentally ill' and the 'sane', since their work rests on a different world view which draws on the observations, thoughts, and writing of earlier psychotherapists as well as writers, film makers and poets. Recognising the physical and psychological harm often created by the 'medical model' they advocate that what's important is establishing a 'good enough' relationship within which therapeutic change can take place.

During my training as a psychotherapist I read extensively about the concepts and the history of psychoaalysis. These early pioneers sought to make sense of the relationship between the mind and body and their work was highly original. I read with interest how Freud's initial friendship with Jung was mutually creative, but eventually that their differences brought an end to their cooperation. I read with scepticism about how Melanie Klein's analysis of children's 'play' contributed to an understanding of aggression and envy. I was entranced with Winnicott's observations on the quality of a baby's relationship with their mother, and his conclusions derived from these observations; that these were fundamental to an adult's resilience and sense of self-worth.

With some astonishment I'd also read how during the Second World War a group of analysts had continued their arguments about theory in a hall in central London, foolishly oblivious to the bombs raining down outside. Only the sanity of Winnicott prevailed. He suggested that perhaps it was wise to set aside the conflict until a later date. As a paediatrician and an analyst, Winnicott's approach to the mother-infant relationship was particularly poetic and gentle, although he remained aware of the more negative and destructive elements of the human psyche.

Each of the above contributed essential concepts to an understanding of both our conscious and unconscious mind and laid the foundations for the psychotherapists and psychoanalysts who followed. Their influence has been immeasurable.

However, putting aside the two perspectives of the 'medical model' versus the 'hermeneutic' or philosophical model of psychotherapy, the general public may also hold a third perspective in their understanding of mental illness. This is slightly different from either the medical or the analytic model of psychotherapy, since it rests on a 'split', the belief that there are only two states of mind; one is sanity, the other madness. Whereas in reality, by which I mean psychic reality, there is a continuum between the two, which can and does change over time and circumstances, according to an individual's situation.

A medical diagnosis is most often based on a number of symptoms which are likely to include hallucinatory or delusional factors, and/or changes in behaviour, an increase in the intensity of emotion such as extreme fear, anger, confusion, anxiety, inability to sleep, and a loss of appetite. Yet, against this, such symptoms can be understood as temporary, and derived from extreme experiences, as with post-traumatic stress disorder. But with specialised and empathic help, it may be argued that these symptoms need not become part of everyday life, thus avoiding a diagnosis of mental illness.

These problems with understanding and formulating a diagnosis are not recent. They go back many years, if not decades, and as an indication of the widespread concern long felt by many professionals, between 1969 and 1972 such difficulties were put to the test.

Known as the 'Rosenhan' experiment, the psychologist, the psychiatrist, and academic Dr Rosenhan together with seven others, all totally sane, adopted false names and identities and presented themselves to various psychiatric hospitals spread across a number of American States. They complained of hallucinations, of hearing strange voices and of experiencing an existential crisis. On this basis alone, every individual was admitted to hospital for psychiatric treatment. Six were diagnosed as schizophrenic and one as suffering with manic depression, now called bi-polar. What were the conclusions of this experiment?

Rosenhan wrote, 'There was a uniform failure to recognize sanity in any of the pseudo patients, and not one of them was ever found out by the hospital staff. The pseudo patients showed no new symptoms and even reported that the strange voices had gone away, yet the doctors and staff continued to believe that their diagnoses were correct.'[21] He further rather chillingly observed that from the time of the diagnosis all behaviour, even the most ordinary and commonplace was from that moment reframed to accord with the medical diagnosis. Yet astonishingly, the actual inpatients had absolutely no problem in recognising the pseudo patients as fake. Perhaps indicating there was 'a sanity in their madness.'

Subsequently, professionals opposed to Dr Rosenhan pointed out that his views were influenced by the work of R.D. Laing[22] and also that the experiment raised a whole range of philosophical and ethical issues. But despite these criticisms, Rosenhan's premise on the difficulties of diagnosing mental illness, and the power of 'labelling' holds true today. His paper 'On Being Sane in Insane Places' even though still seen as controversial, continues to be powerfully relevant.[23]

To be classified as 'mentally ill' today, is not equivalent to being diagnosed with say, appendicitis or meningitis. It is not a physical illness with a clearly identified cause, and as critics of the powerful DSM have noted the financial interests of the big Insurance companies also have a vested interest in maintaining a belief in the validity of the medical diagnosis.[24]

For example, when considering schizophrenia or bi-polar; generally speaking the symptoms of either, are often, if not usually, reported in terms of violent or outlandish behaviour. Depression on

---

21 David. L. Rosenhan, 'On Being Sane in Insane Places', *Science,* 179(4070): 250-258, 1973.
22 See Chapter 11 in this book.
23 David. L. Rosenhan, 1973.
24 See Chapter 1 in this book and Stijn Vanheule. *Diagnosis and the DSM: A Critical Review*. Palgrave Macmillan, 2014.

the other hand, is seen as totally disabling, incomprehensible, and an extreme reaction to experiences and feelings we all may have experienced at some time. The general public however, may understand all these states of mind as permanent.

To return to one of the opening sections of this book called 'A Conversation about Therapy' (Chapter 3), Harry had been diagnosed as depressed which had developed from a situation over which he had no control. Despite this, it is noticeable, when talking of depression, a typical response, besides often expressing a total lack of empathy, will often carry some disapproval, or worse, the hint of a value judgement as indicated by Emily's response to Harry's depression. Harry had voluntarily disclosed that his father had been killed in a fatal road accident and that, as a result, his mother was permanently disabled. Consequently, he was obliged to be her carer and thus relive the consequences of this life changing accident, alone, and on a daily basis.

His history accords with what many psychotherapists know, depression often indicates a major loss or a type of ongoing trauma which at some point in a patient's life leaves in its wake, feelings of abandonment, anger, confusion, and anxiety about themselves and the purpose of life.

In contrast to this approach, that is one in which a psychotherapist would include a 'real event' in a patient's assessment with all its consequent thoughts and feelings, in comparison a 'mental illness' as diagnosed by a member of the medical profession usually rests on the biological as a primary cause. And understanding what may have preceded, if not caused, the problem, is not part of the analysis.

While acknowledging the 'medical model' may contain an environmental or a psychological element to the diagnosis, patients categorised in this way are likely to be treated with various types of psychotropic medication. These affect mood, perception and energy levels with the possibility of long term dependency and highly unpleasant neurological problems as for example, weight gain, anxiety, and blurred vision. Additionally, where there is a danger of harm to themselves and others, such patients may be subject to incarceration, usually referred to as being 'sectioned'. The 'section' being the part of the Mental Health Act legitimising this action.

A quick glance at recent scientific research into possible causes for the development of schizophrenia down plays the notion of hereditary factors and stresses the importance of the environment, particularly the early environment. By environment it means the relationships and experiences of family life; maternal care, the presence or absence of a father figure, economic structural issues of poverty or affluence, chance factors; loss, accidents, illness, birth, and lifestyle choices such as the desire for fame. Such issues within a family were regarded as particularly important by Laing and many others. These may indicate the origin of a patient's confusion derived from the quality, the lack of openness, understanding, thought and trust between family members.

For example, for some years I had been working with Polly, a patient who had been sexually abused as a young child by a neighbour. Consequently, she had a multitude of emotions, many of which were based on her memories and fears of the past, but overall she experienced them as conflicting, transient, and frightening. She was desperate to be loved, but could not trust. She had no experience of being thought about or cared for. She felt dirty and repellent and often felt that the abuse was her fault. She blamed herself for the abuse, saying she should have known the neighbour's behaviour was wrong and stopped him. Her mother meanwhile seemed oblivious to her daughter's abuse and when her daughter eventually attempted to tell her, she refused to listen and recognise her distress.

If we think about the dominant figures in Polly's childhood, we have an uncaring and neglectful mother, an absent father, who is rarely referred to, and an exploitative and abusive neighbour. Within a session, any of these people may metaphorically appear in some way or another and her feelings about each of them became projected onto myself as her therapist. When this occurred, Polly saw me as if I was the absent father, the neglectful mother, or the potential abuser. Her point of view derived from her experience, i.e. why else would I be interested in her? She had no alternative history of care or thoughtfulness to draw upon. It was these unspoken thoughts which often lay behind her distrust of me and the confused way she saw herself and others.

At such moments communication became difficult. With great care, words had to be found which could contain Polly's distress and confusion. These would enable her to differentiate between her fears of the past and the reality of the present. But this could occur only within a long term relationship based on trust and mutual understanding within the therapeutic relationship.

Being diagnosed as 'mentally ill', whether as schizophrenic, bi-polar, or depressed, is almost always associated with extreme fear, whether that of the recipient or of the public. The public's expectation of unpredictable and strange behaviour, creates an equally strong reaction on behalf of those classified in this way. They feel isolated, judged, diminished, misunderstood, belittled and stigmatised. Given this societal reaction, it is no surprise that individuals withdraw from relationships and friendships. This invariably increases the intensity of their symptoms and feelings of being dangerously different from the rest of society.

Thus it can be argued that the public contributes in some ways to these feelings of madness, even though unintentional. It may also be said, perhaps more controversially, that their own madness has become invested in the other. By which there is a split between those seen as mad and those sane—that they are different people (e.g. 'he is mad but I am sane.') Within sociology, this is understood by the term 'labelling theory', a concept also used by Rosenhan.

'Labelling theory' derives originally from the research of Howard Becker, an American Sociologist working in Chicago in the 1960s who, observing the actions and life styles of those seen as deviant, which included the mentally ill, wrote their self and identity had developed in response to how they were seen and judged.[25] Similarly Goffman's research and observations of those incarcerated in a psychiatric hospital, comments that the identity of

25 Howard S. Becker, *Outsiders: Studies in the Sociology of Deviance*. Free Press, 1963.

such patients develops as a response to how medical staff perceive them.[26] An observation powerfully made elsewhere in this book by Dr Morton Schatzman (Chapter 11). And, from my own experience, having worked at some point with those classified as 'mentally ill' (bi-polar) it hadn't escaped me that there was often a 'performance element' to their lives. It was as if, at some level, they knew there was an expectation to prove how exciting, unpredictable and out of control their lives were in comparison to our own.

Additionally my own research which had focused on talking with children placed on a Care Order (for being dangerously angry and out of control I discovered that the actual reasons for their behaviour seemed to lie with the parents.

I had asked the children to talk about punishment. They spoke about getting smacked, hit, headbutted, sworn at, shouted at, whacked round the face, being kept in. Punishment, it was clear, was very common and given for swearing, shouting, not listening, bringing 'dirt' into the house. Not one child mentioned a close and loving relationship with an adult.[27]

Thus deviant behaviour, as argued by the labelling theorists, is a consequence of certain actions being classified within a set of written and unwritten rules, which have laid down expectations of behaviour. A failure to conform leads to the label of 'deviancy' or the development of certain personality characteristics which may pass as 'normal'.

A further example from my own work as a psychotherapist seems to confirm this perspective; but ultimately a therapeutic intervention prevented potential rule-breaking behaviour from escalating into a deviant act.

A troubled patient of mine came into her session very upset. She began telling me how on the way to see me, passengers on a bus were talking about her. She thought they saw her as weird. I

---

26 Erving Goffman, *Asylums: Essays on the Social Situation of Mental Patients and Other Inmates*. Doubleday, 1961.
27 Marguerite Mary Valentine, *Developing a Critical Theory of Child Abuse as a Manifestation of the Social Order*. PhD Thesis University of Warwick, 1989. https://wrap.warwick.ac.uk/34822

had no idea whether this was true or not, but we discussed various and different explanations. My response seemed to calm her, as she said, 'Talking with you makes me feel normal and better'. Paranoia was avoided here by working with her on understanding her own feelings, so eventually she was able to see the judgement she made about how she thought she was seen, possibly originated from within herself (and perhaps from within her family of origin).

The term, 'projective identification' is a classic psychoanalytic concept, first developed by Melanie Klein, a close colleague of Freud. Laing, a psychiatrist and a gifted interpreter of madness, also used this notion in his analysis of communication between members of seriously disturbed families. Projective identification is understood as the transmission of intense feelings or thoughts between two people. Within a therapy session, it's similar to transference and countertransference but ratcheted up many times. It's a fundamental communication from the unconscious, since it often indicates thoughts, feelings and phantasies which remain unknown, disturbing and therefore cannot be verbalised in a straight forward way. It is part of the work of the therapist to interpret and to find words for these unspoken fears.

Richard Beard's recent memoir *Sad Little Men* explores in excoriating detail the impact on the hearts and minds of young boys abandoned by their not so well meaning parents to an English Public School education.[28] He documents in fine and careful detail the impact such a system has, not only on the individual but also ultimately on the government of this country. For example, he notes that in Thatcher's first Cabinet, ninety-one per cent were male and private school educated and observes that this emphasis on class and financial background in the upper echelons of government continues to this day. Perhaps such experiences are particularly British, but if so, why should this matter?

It matters because such an education has instilled in the ex-public school individual the notion of 'rightful' privilege, a disdain, if not contempt towards those less fortunate, and a strong

---

28 Richard Beard, *Sad Little Men: How Public Schools Failed Britain*. Vintage, 2021.

belief in their own exceptionalism (i.e. rules and regulations are for others, not themselves). This is even more apparent today as anyone with the slightest interest in politics will have observed, which was particularly true during Brexit and throughout the Covid years. As I write, it is becoming more and more obvious even to those who have little knowledge or interest in politics, that the present government's commitment to increasing the life chances for the better is skewed wholly to their own socio-economic class.

Apart from these characteristics, the author also observed the emotional impact on boys separated from their parents at an early age. They have learnt to survive in a harsh and punitive environment and writing of his own experience, he says 'we were like cockroaches, tough shelled and invincible, rubbish at expressions of joy, but world class at emotional and physical suffering … we were expected to endure and to make endurance a habit.'

In this and elsewhere, Richard Beard in observing the impact of a public school education on young boys' minds, points to the development of a particular type of personality; one which is comprised of an inability to form close relationships, a lack of empathy or compassion towards suffering, limited understanding of others, and a split between thought and feeling. These characteristics, developed as a defence against loss, depression, and childhood experiences of authoritarianism are typical of a 'schizoid' personality (note, these characteristics are not related to diagnosis of schizophrenia). Unsurprisingly, these characteristics are unlikely to be categorised as a 'mental illness', since they may be seen as necessary and even an admirable characteristic in certain occupations, and therefore have become 'normalised'.

For example, George Monbiot's recent book on the negative if not destructive impact of the development of the 'market' which he analyses in terms of the ideological forces of 'neoliberalism' can also be understood as having a profound influence on the national psyche.[29]

---

29 George Monbiot and Peter Hutchison, *The Invisible Doctrine: The Secret History of Neoliberalism (& How It Came to Control Your Life)*. Penguin Books, 2024. See Chapter 1.

When working with a level of disturbance which may be unsettling, things are not necessarily what they seem, which is one of the points about a 'talking therapy'. It differs from an ordinary conversation. Knowing what a story, a phrase, or an event might really mean requires skill, imagination, and a good memory. Both the therapist and the person in therapy need an ability to listen, to reflect, to rise above the noise and sometimes the deluge of words, which serves only to conceal what a person really feels or searches to understand. Only then is it possible to find some psychic space where the well-timed phrase or observation may lead to a useful insight.

Laing comments having observed a conversation between two or more, it appears as if nothing is going on. Everything seems normal, but in time, the observer may notice for example, how trivia tends to be the main topic of all conversation. He may wonder why, and even if it has an important function. But this apparently innocent preoccupation with trivia, definitely does have a role. It confuses and acts like a decoy in diverting attention from what really is important.

The end result is, as Laing observes, that many 'borderline' and 'schizophrenic' patients are puzzled by what is really meant and what is really going on. They perceive a conversation as open to many interpretations. They ask of themselves how can such a conversation be understood, what does it really mean, is it about them or me? Ultimately they may become profoundly confused and over time, this can result in a corrosive anxiety and with feelings of being conned.

In *The Divided Self* Laing wrote that when he certifies that someone is insane, that they need the special care and the attention of a mental hospital, he is also aware that 'there are other people … whose minds are as radically unsound, who may be equally or more dangerous to themselves and others and whom society does not regard as psychotic and fit persons to be in a madhouse … and I am aware that the man who is said to be deluded may in his delusion be telling the truth'.[30]

---

30 R. D. Laing, *The Divided Self: An Existential Study in Sanity and Madness*, p. 27. Pelican, 1964.

— CHAPTER 17 —

The Challenge of the Crisis Centre

In 1973 Arbours opened the 'Crisis Centre' which aimed to provide immediate residential support and help to those experiencing sudden mental and social breakdown. Based in North London, it was large enough to offer accommodation for seven guests, with additional space for psychotherapists and administration. It was a physically containing environment, and one that lent itself to the necessary multiple, overlapping and interweaving support and clinical spaces. The interior had space and light, with views over the carefully tended garden with mature trees.

The staff consisted of three resident psychotherapists, a number of highly experienced psychotherapists who worked on an ad hoc basis as team leaders, and a trainee psychotherapist. Regular consultations with a psychiatrist were also available. Referrals typically were self-referrals, or from general practitioners, social workers, and psychiatrists.

The residents of the Crisis Centre often came with a long history of disturbing personal and interpersonal problems. Typically they would have experienced various types of medication, irregular and unsuccessful stays in a psychiatric hospital, and although coming from all walks of life, they shared similar feelings of hopelessness, despair, anger, and anxiety. This history usually went along with the expectation that nothing had helped or could help and they were incapable of ever feeling better.

The following are two accounts of the work undertaken with such patients; the first by Steve, called 'Thinking Allowed', was written while working in the Crisis Centre as a residential psychotherapist. The second, 'Night Time Terrors', was written by myself during my time as a trainee. Both accounts are based on actual notes and discussions taken at the time. All identifying facts have been changed to protect anonymity.

— CHAPTER 18 —

Steve on 'Thinking Allowed'

The emotional demands of challenging behaviour can be draining. To understand extreme anxiety and confusion, it is imperative that the therapist gets 'up close and personal'. The aim being to see and experience the world from the patient's point of view. While helpful, this has its dangers in that the merging may become symbiotic and the therapist needs some help to disentangle themselves.

Defining 'boundaries' in such work is essential. In all the patients described here, the need for boundaries became particularly important in terms of defining what behaviour could be tolerated or more subtly, to develop the awareness of the internal boundary within the therapist's mind between the psychotic and non-psychotic part.

A second fundamental point is the necessity for supervision. This must take place frequently, both individually and as a team with an experienced supervisor. Often the supervision takes place in separate premises outside the Crisis Centre. The literal space of a separate room seemed to free up thinking and this was particularly true when 'splitting' between teams or within a team occurred as in the cases discussed here.

Therapist's Observations

A few weeks into my placement a thirty-five-year-old woman by the name of Jane and chaperoned by her brother, arrived. She had agreed to stay for a period of assessment from an earlier visit when they turned up unannounced on the doorstep. For the previous five years or so Jane had been hospitalised, medicated, and then allowed her freedom. As long as her medication was taken, all would appear to be fine, but usually within months of leaving hospital, and convinced that medication was not required as she was no longer ill, Jane ceased taking it.

Her behaviour then became increasingly erratic, her moods volatile. Her growing omnipotence and paranoia rendered her unpredictable and anxiety-provoking for those around her, especially her family. The family would struggle with her as her grip on reality loosened, and eventually she would be hospitalised again. This pattern had occurred each year for the previous five years. We also discovered there was a history of earlier psychiatric intervention, from when she was aged eighteen.

Jane was a charismatic, intelligent, well-educated woman with high levels of functionality and at times very sophisticated interpersonal skills. Sometimes in conversation or interaction with her it was easy to forget that she was unwell. She would sometimes speak, or rather orate, with such confidence and conviction in her delivery, I felt she could rally an army to war. Often in her presence I would experience the urge to dance.

Other times I felt like a dismissed manservant. I felt a strong sense of commitment to her and wanted to help and end this painful suffering she'd endured for so long. As there had been uncertainty about her precise arrival date, it had been agreed I would be her residential psychotherapist along with one of the Team Leaders. We agreed initially to meet with her three times per week within an assessment period of eight weeks. (This later increased to five times per week).

Initially things proceeded well. Jane appeared to settle down and engage with the other guests in the House albeit with a slight inclination to spend time on her own either in or out of the House. Over the Christmas period, she had said she wanted to return to her home to see her children and although concerned about the risk of her ceasing her medication whilst being away from the Crisis Centre, this was eventually agreed. Jane further persuasively convinced me and the Team Leader that following her eight week assessment, if she were to come back and spend more time here, the therapeutic goal would be to reduce her medication to an optimum level. Her hope was that this might lead over time, to none at all.

We did not dismiss this idea, nor offer any assurances that we would do this. However, I found myself becoming increasingly excited at the prospect. Sharing my thoughts with the Team Leader, I said that this is what the Crisis Centre stood for and it was perhaps the only place left in the UK where this was possible. It provided the necessary structure, both physical and more importantly psychological, to hold, contain, and facilitate such change.

In my mind I was positioning Jane as a victim of gender and of an unjust and Dickensian medical system that had and still was failing her. I further fantasised that we at the Crisis Centre were offering her a unique opportunity to liberate herself of these cruel and oppressive regimes that had so dominated her past, and that her quality of life could improve.

These hopes were not shared. When we spoke in the Clinical Meeting of our hopes of a gradual reduction with the intention of possibly stopping Jane's medication, we were met with resistance. This eventually led to 'splitting' and some highly charged emotions within the staff group. Over time this led to the Team Leader and myself, feeling extremely isolated. The staff group, the cover staff and even my fellow RTs questioned the wisdom of what we were trying to achieve with Jane.

Additionally, in the absence of our usual psychiatrist we were obliged to secure an external psychiatrist on a locum basis. However, as an outsider and new to the workings of the Crisis Centre, we were concerned he could not possibly grasp how we were attempting to work with Jane. Consequently I was bitterly disappointed, but not surprised when the psychiatrist took, to me, what seemed to be a very conventional and conservative position with regards to reducing medication. The whole experience was frustrating and fundamentally at odds with our thinking.

Subsequently, feeling isolated from the wider group, the Team Leader and I attempted to understand the consequences of our thinking. We saw the work with Jane as creative, challenging, and potentially exciting, but it seemed problematic in relation to the other staff and the guest group. Also I wondered how these issues had impacted upon Jane.

However, after this initial assessment period of eight weeks Jane did return to her family for the Christmas break. We had planned that she return in January for an as yet unspecified period, but given the hopes I had for her, I was thinking a minimum of two years.

Meanwhile, Jane's departure in the third week of December left me with the responsibility for another guest whom I shall call Mary. After three years stay in a hospital, Mary had arrived at the Crisis Centre a year or so before me, and her therapist left a month before I arrived. Mary, I observed, was consumed with envy. If she witnessed others getting along with each other she found this excruciatingly painful. A typical response by Mary to this unbearable pain, would be to take a knife from the kitchen drawer and press it into her throat, occasionally drawing blood whilst threatening to kill herself. It was convincing and frightening to witness. It was tempting to be pulled into this drama without thinking.

But I also noted that the response from others appeared monitored by Mary. Her appraisal for each situation depended on who was around. Given this, it seemed to the team, her behaviour was an unconscious attack on thinking. This developed in the presence of those of us, who, for whatever reason at any given time, were unable to think. The quicker and more urgent the (unthinking) action, the more likely Mary was to put the knife into her throat, and thus create by way of response, an extreme anxiety in the other.

Additionally, infant-like projectile vomiting and outbursts of flatulence had become commonplace in the Crisis Centre which may tell us something of the primitive and preverbal landscapes being explored. Mary seemed to act out 'Kleinian' theory literally, such were the often 'concrete' nature of her projections. These occurred at the very moment that something could not be taken in, or tolerated by her. Her obsessive thinking—which she later came to recognise and name as 'the motor', seemed to serve as a defence against the horrors of separation. Accordingly, much of the therapeutic work with her was to show by our actions and words that we had a separate mind from her, and that we could contain her anxiety within it.

However, her rage-fuelled tantrums, both in and outside the Teams were exhausting. In one Team meeting, following a moment where I was silently and resolutely refusing to collude with her, the rising anxiety took on an unbearably threatening quality, Mary stood up and stood over me. I was convinced she might well hit me, but I resolutely held my position. Instead she just bellowed like a bull elephant at me and with such murderous conviction that she might as well have hit me.

I felt psychologically and physically bruised by her outburst. I believe that in that moment my own internal conviction not to collude, met with something in her, that I needed to be separate and show her this. A boundary was established.

During one fairly typical evening, following what seemed like hours of increasing input to contain Mary, the atmosphere became evermore threatening. Mary had taken to launching objects across the room, and each one came dangerously close to hitting a member of staff. Sitting next to the member of cover staff, I asked Mary what was going on.

Mary was clearly distressed, but also seemed to be enjoying the power of her threatening and menacing behaviour. At this point, I realised we had to some extent been walking on eggshells around her, allowing each outcry, screech or bang to get louder without intervening—an absurdity in itself, to 'pretend' that nothing was happening. I felt inside and not for the first time, a growing anger that I was being controlled.. She was immensely and increasingly intimidating and we, it seemed, were powerless to stop her doing anything she liked. I don't know if it occurred to me then or later in a thoughtful way, or if I was just being intuitive, but I decided to communicate my thoughts to her.

I said I could clearly see that she was very distressed and I asked her what she wanted. She responded by pushing a heavy wooden table across the floor in an aggressive way.

'Ah, you want to destroy everything.' I said.

'Yes I do!' she yelled. 'I want to smash up the whole house!'

The word 'house' came with a long drawn out scream. I began to wonder if I ought not to have engaged with her in this way, and that I'd made things worse. I was scared now that she was going to absolutely lose all self-control, yet at the same time I sensed she was actually terrified of losing her mind.

'OK, and then what?' I said, hoping that she would not recognise the fear now in me. 'What do you think is going to happen, after that?'

She paused momentarily; just long enough for me to believe that part of her did care, before shouting back that she didn't care! The focus was on me now and I realised that this is what she wanted; the undivided attention of another. The member of cover staff had withdrawn after the table had been shoved across the room. Mary wanted and needed at that point to have a direct connection with another. The emotional arousal established an authentic connection for both of us and I was keen to maintain this.

I said, 'You know what? I can see that you're really upset and if you really want to smash up this house, go ahead and knock yourself out. I'm not going to stop you, but tomorrow it will have to be paid for.'

I said this in a way that I meant it. Being prepared to persevere in the face of relentless torrents of abuse, month after month after month, and not give in to the pull to action is what made the difference. She was exhausting to be with and yet there was something also immensely tragic in her suffering.

After Christmas, Jane returned. It was a week later than planned. We hadn't seen her like this before. She was omnipotent, emphatic and tyrannical, although in the team she could be rational and coherent. Was she protecting us from her anguish? Others in the House were fearful and resentful of her presence. I too had serious doubts about our ability to contain Jane. Yet it was necessary, as we realised that the fear, resentment and sense of being controlled, were largely her unwanted projections.

In addition there was further splitting, and within the staff group and the team, there were strong feelings regarding the use of her medication. Some colleagues were for no change to medication. I was still for reducing to optimum use and close monitoring, but this would entail continuing to bear the sometimes excruciating levels of anxiety. I also observed that when faced with extremely disturbing and psychotic behaviour, some are naturally drawn to the medical model. In practice this appears to primarily relieve their own anxieties, as well as protect Jane from the horrifying anguish and torment that seemed to dominate her inner world.

Many things were at play for me in this clinically isolating experience and no doubt, among other things, my need to be the best residential psychotherapist and the one who saved Jane where so many had failed. My own narcissism, in other words, was lurking somewhere in the bitter mix. But also important, the thought that we have to look after ourselves and recognise our own limitations. But when clinical thinking does become stuck or polarised it's helpful to find a third position or a place from which fresh thinking can emerge. In other words it becomes necessary to think about the thinking.

Thus, following a period of harrowing and verbally aggressive behaviour from Jane, we rather reluctantly arranged a visit to the local Psychiatric Hospital. We were told, she would be seen for a Mental Health Assessment by a senior and experienced psychiatrist. Our concerns were that Jane would abscond, but on the other hand if she was admitted, in the long run this wouldn't influence events either way.

I attended the assessment with Jane but to my amazement she presented in a calm, intelligent, reasonable way. I could hardly believe this sea change in Jane's presentation. We had not made this call to the hospital lightly, and I was really pleased that she had escaped admission. However, on returning to the Crisis Centre triumphantly, I was astounded at the shock, horror and disappointment of some of the other staff who could hardly contain their fury at me for 'failing to get her sectioned'. One residential psychotherapist actually left the building and did not speak to me for a long time, such was her disappointment.

On another occasion following a very difficult and protracted attempt to negotiate with Jane to attend the Mental Health Assessment appointment, we were on our way in an ambulance to the hospital, when the driver was contacted and told Jane could not attend and would not be assessed! Again I witnessed at first hand the difficulties that the Crisis Centre had in its working relations with external organisations.

We felt like an isolated mother with little or no support. The psychotic projections, irrespective of source and origin seemed to know no bounds and everyone it seemed had become drawn in. Although in reality I have no idea whether this was a shared experienced, it just felt so at the time. The sense of isolation and abandonment for me was as if we were in a submarine miles away from the most northern Russian coastline, deep in the freezing ocean. Completely isolated, lost, and forgotten, forever. The impact of psychotic projections on those working closely in such environments cannot be underestimated.

Not long after these experiences, I was in the Studio for a session of dance movement therapy with a guest called Hannah. Hannah was a postgraduate at Oxbridge and had high levels of functionality. For example, we might go to the cinema or a meal but during that time, I became aware of a pull to confide in her. I found this very seductive. Her astonishing ability to convince others that she was fine, at times when she was in fact acutely fragile, ensured that others often believed her at the very moment she most needed to be seen. In house meetings, Hannah could, if she had chosen, almost become the fourth residential therapist, since she demonstrated an impressive tolerance and understanding of the other guests.

However, on one particular session of Hannah's dance therapy, she had become speechless and was crouched on the floor holding a blanket wrapped around her. The look on her face told me she was present but I would be lucky to find her. In remembering this moment an image springs to mind, of shining a torch into Hannah's eyes and finding in her interior world, a much smaller frightened Hannah, hiding behind a rock.

I felt strongly in that moment that Hannah had come to the dance movement for something unknown and incapable of being verbalised. I knelt beside her, feeling compelled to demonstrate a solidarity and alliance to her; silently hoping she would come out from behind that rock, and yet also feeling at ease if she didn't. The Dance movement therapist, whom I had not seen for several weeks because of the Christmas break, noticed that change in me. With considerable concern, and with remarkable clinical stealth, she facilitated the disentanglement of me from my Guest's state of mind.

She sensed I was straddling both worlds, seemingly between the psychotic and the non-psychotic. By trying to understand, she seemed concerned if not baffled, by my lack of response. I remember also losing a sense of time and for one and a half hours, I didn't speak, but the dance therapist found a way of responding. Her words were thoughtfully chosen, and breathing slowly and cautiously as if diffusing a bomb, she somehow conveyed her intent to understand and to help.

I also noticed at some point that Hannah's attention had shifted from her internal world to noticing my being with her. I felt her awareness of my presence was somehow acknowledged. At the same time I was conscious of a recognition of something powerful which I don't normally experience. This was the bliss of relinquishing all and any responsibility for anything, anymore. I was submerged in this experience, or my fantasy of the experience, of forming a psychological alliance with my guest.

Some time later I found myself sitting opposite my Team Leader. She looked at me and made no attempt to disguise her shock. 'Are you okay?' she asked, and I could see the look of concern on her face.

In that moment I felt both relieved and angry that she was aware of how disturbed I felt. It was a profound moment for me. I said, 'Well I don't think I am okay actually.'

It took a few hours for me to come back to normal. I felt I had experienced a very disturbed state of mind. It was attractive. I had experienced the power. I knew that it was self-destructive. If I had stayed with it, I wouldn't have been able to come back. Since then, I have becom increasingly convinced that it is the relationship we have with the other, which makes the difference between whether we succumb to the exquisite seduction of psychosis or choose to stay with the misery of reality. The words from a Bob Dylan song seem to capture something of this experience: 'You lose yourself. You reappear ... they really found you.'[31]

---

[31] Bob Dylan, 'It's Alright Ma (I'm Only Bleeding), 1964. 'It's Alright Ma (I'm Only Bleeding). https://www.bobdylan.com/songs/its-alright-ma-im-only-bleeding

— CHAPTER 19 —

Marguerite on 'Night Time Terrors'

Patients who cut and burn themselves are particularly distressing for the therapist. By harming their body they have replaced words as the primary mode of therapeutic communication. This may be understood as an unconscious attack on the therapeutic process, but paradoxically the action of self-harm is also a cry of despair for care and understanding. Here the psychic challenges on the therapist are considerable and most often need the support of an experienced supervisor.

The following discussion considers some of these issues. Winnicott's comments in his brilliant paper, 'Hate in the Counter Transference' are particularly helpful.[32] He compares such challenging moments with those of a desperately tired mother. At times, she feels driven by hatred for her baby who ruthlessly refuses to respond to her care, but finds she can do nothing other than tolerate his behaviour.

---

32 Donald W Winnicott, 'Hate in the Counter-Transference'. *Journal of Psychotherapy Practice and Research,* Fall; 3(4): 348-56, 1994. Originally published in *The International Journal of Psycho-Analysis*, 30: 69-74, 1949.

On such occasions, it is essential for the therapist to become aware of their own hate and desperation for their patient, who remains oblivious to the depth of feeling within the therapist. Interpretations at such times must be postponed. Winnicott writes, 'It is important to study the ways in which anxiety of a psychotic quality and also hate are produced in those who work with severely ill psychiatric patients. Only in this way can there be any hope of the avoidance of therapy that is adapted to the needs of the therapist rather than to the needs of the patient.' (For a similar point made by Carl Jung see Chapter 4.) The fundamental point is the necessity for the therapist's own hate to be experienced, understood and contained before love can develop.

Therapist's Observations

Was it a coincidence that her mother had called her Layla, a name associated with the night, or that I had always been an admirer of Anne Sexton's poem 'Her Kind' in which she writes, 'I have gone out, a possessed witch, haunting the black air, braver at night; dreaming evil.'[33]

The truth is that before even meeting Layla, and as a member of the Crisis Centre team designated to work with her, I was both fascinated and horrified by what I knew of her. Her reputation had preceded her and it was with some trepidation that the team at the Crisis Centre which consisted of a team leader, a residential therapist and myself, waited for her arrival. She was late, the delay apparently due to her barrister's argument at the court hearing, that to avoid a possible prison sentence, she would benefit from psychotherapy.

Layla was already no stranger to therapy having earlier developed an obsession with her counsellor. This took the form of her taking to the streets late at night, and there positioning herself in the bushes surrounding the counsellor's house she kept watch through the night. Sometimes she'd fall asleep and later, after we had got to

---

33 See https://www.poetryfoundation.org/poems/42560/her-kind

know each other, Layla had told me that on one occasion knowing the counsellor was away, she'd broken into her house, eaten food from the fridge, read through her personal papers, and fallen asleep in her bed. Intrigued, I had asked whether she ever felt fear and she'd pointed with some pride to her boots, and said, 'They're Doc Martens, steel capped, safety boots for work.'

The image of her alone, hiding in the bushes and sleeping outside in the dark, captured my imagination and it also must be said, appealed to the delinquent side of me. I wondered how her behaviour could be understood. The act seemed to me to represent totally contradictory elements of her personality; on the one hand aggression and indifference to the other's fear, and on the other, her vulnerability and desperate search for care and acceptance. Or to put it another way, she was both the predator and the wounded, desperately searching for maternal care to heal her psychic wounds.

The day she was expected at the Crisis Centre came and went. We heard that she'd been 'bound over to keep the peace' and could come any time but we had no idea when. Not knowing when, or if, she was coming seemed a powerful way to start her stay. But just as we were discussing her non-arrival and wondering whether the lateness was due to her ambivalence, the front door bell rang. It was 6.15 p.m.

I had expected without thinking too much about it, a small, fragile person, in other words, the wounded Layla, but what I saw was anything but. She was pretty, of medium height, thin, pale and gaunt, her black hair braided, and dressed in a baggy, old, leather jacket with tracksuit bottoms. She wore heavy, masculine style boots and had a ring in her nose and several through each ear. Her appearance was one of unkempt aggression.

The team leader said, after greeting her, and sitting her down in the therapy room, that the three of us would work with her during her stay and that this time was set aside as one of several therapy sessions for her. We would meet on a regular weekly basis. Layla's response was to cry, her distress seeming to contradict her persona and history but, it seemed to me her tears were genuine and not designed to manipulate us. She told us she hadn't really wanted to come, she'd been in prison, and there'd been some 'mess-up' getting her funding for her stay at Arbours. She was angry. She said she'd felt pushed around and although it might have been horrible in prison, at least she felt safe. She had thought and expected Arbours wouldn't want her and covering her bowed head with her hands she apologised for her tears.

This gesture of covering her bent head with her hands we were to observe several times during her stay. It put in my mind a small child protecting her head from the blows of an angry and physically abusive parent.

The team leader said, 'You know, Arbours is able to offer you a different kind of care. The meetings will always be at the same time and with ourselves, and these might also give you some experience of safety.'

Following this first meeting we had discussed Layla's comment on the prison offering her safety. We saw it as an indication of her awareness of a need to 'contain' her sense of danger. This concept of 'containment' which we understood as a psychic need was to become an overriding issue in our work with Layla. Containers can be empty or full and they also have boundaries which separate the inside from the outside. The skin is also a boundary and separates one person from another. Layla, we discovered, did not like to see an empty container. For example, if she saw an empty bowl or a cup, she would immediately place it upside down. It was as if the empty container was in some way a vivid and unbearable symbol of her own emptiness.

Linked with this was her demand for 'hugs'. Although she had never stated that a hug could make her feel safe (contained) it was fairly clear that this was her unconscious intention. She had hoped that a hug would make her feel better, but found that this didn't work, so wanted more. She wanted hugs without having to ask for them and saw this as proof she was loved and cared for. Her wearing of a big, baggy, leather jacket, which didn't fit was also indicative of her state of mind. She did not truly live in her own skin.

It became apparent she had no boundaries and my experience of her was of a fluid nature. My feelings about her ebbed and flowed, sometimes, as I got to know her more, crystallised into a terror of her potentially unmitigated violence and her malevolent invasiveness. Sometimes I felt a tenderness for her vulnerability and hurt. Overall, I felt 'full up', she was just too much, and this led to feelings of being 'fed up.' Yet, despite this ambivalence I wanted to understand her and to also develop with her, a therapeutic alliance of 'containment'. Once I communicated this to the team leader, it was agreed. The two of us would daily spend an hour together but how we spent that time, was left open.

Layla had numerous fears. These were about suicide, her anger with Arbours, her deep resentment for the various counsellors who once they had got to know her, would try and get her 'sectioned' or call the police. Then she felt abandoned and let down. She began telling me in more detail about her stalking. She advised me never see anyone in my home because, 'You just don't what you're letting yourself in for.'

She told me she wanted to get into her counsellor's head because she said, she had something that she wanted, and she had a right to that. I suggested that through her actions and words, her fears were transferred into the counsellor (a process called projective identification) to which she replied, she hadn't realised that, until she'd seen how frightened the counsellor was in Court. That she said, had made her feel powerful.

It seemed inevitable that the constant references to her stalking would also get into our heads or under our skin, but either way she was psychically invasive, a state of mind we found profoundly disturbing. For example, she let it be known that she knew more about us than we knew, and as a consequence of that, all three of us had taken to looking over our shoulders One morning my fears seemed realised. A plant had been uprooted and the 'for sale notice' had been ripped from the wall of the house where I lived. It could have been just an act of vandalism, but the next day after I placed the notice out of sight, the following night it was laid out like a javelin on the front steps, the tip pointing at the glass panels in the front door. The message seemed clear enough. It symbolised an intention to break in.

As her team, we felt placed in a 'double bind' since to confront her with our fears could easily be experienced as accusatory. We were therapists, not the police. Therefore for the moment it was left open and remained a subject inaccessible for discussion for the time being. However, soon this was to change in a dramatic and unexpected way. The mother of the residential psychotherapist became very ill, which meant without notice, the therapist had to leave to care for her. There was also the possibility she could not return.

This had a disastrous effect on Layla. Two team meetings later, she told us she thought she was going mad. She said she felt like throwing herself under a tube or out of a window. She looked tortured, twisting her hands and locking her fingers together, moving her head up and down with her eyes closed and her body contorted. She said these feelings began when she was four; the fear of vomiting. She didn't want to vomit, so she developed rituals as a technique to control the vomiting. The ritual was to pray and the more she prayed, the more she felt this could control the fear within her. It worked until she was twelve, but from then on she had to spend more and more time praying. Sometimes she spent five or six hours on the rituals which stopped her socialising and having a normal life.

One week later, we are told the residential therapist was definitely not returning. Layla begins cutting. She apologised to me but then smiled in a sinister way, saying it's time to play games. She'd been thinking of one of the male therapists whom she thought she could shock, but on the other hand, there was someone else in the Crisis Centre who was, she said, 'maternal enough'.

We were sitting in her bedroom when she tells me she had secretly heated a knife in a gas flame in the kitchen and holding the knife against her skin, it had burnt it into her flesh. She pulls her sleeve down to show me.

It's a deep wound. Its effect on me is profound. I am shocked but also feel revulsion at this visible sign of what seems to me, her hatred for her body.

I say, 'Layla, why? Why do you do this to yourself?'

She doesn't answer straight away. Then she says, 'I'm sorry … I regret it. I wished I hadn't.' She turns away so I can't see her face.

'But what's driving you?' She remains silent. I continue, 'Layla, I want to know … tell me. Tell me why you want to hurt yourself. I don't understand.'

She turns towards me but avoiding my eyes, she says, 'I felt tense. Cutting and burning helps. It's a ritual that keeps away the pain.'

I'm thinking that she is incapable of thinking through and of tolerating and containing her psychic pain, so she replaces that with a real, physical pain. Perhaps that way it seems more under her control, or it's a way of punishing herself? But I don't understand this motivation.

Interrupting my thoughts Layla continues with a chilling comment, she says, 'It's time to play again. The more I burn myself, the more care I'll get.'

I pause, I desperately want to reach out to her. I'm well aware of the perverse aggression that her statement carries but I'm still trying to make a connection with her.

'You know that that won't work. Cutting and burning … all it shows is your own self-hatred and how desperate you feel. But you don't need to do that. We do care about you … you don't have to attack yourself.'

My words feel empty. She avoids looking at me. There is no emotional link. I'm aware of the silence in the room and of an overwhelming sense of isolation. She has constructed an impenetrable wall of indifference but at the same time, I am aware of the enormous conflict within her; the well of vulnerability, her feelings of hopelessness, and above all, her cold rage.

Later, talking through this behaviour with the team leader, we wonder whether the residential therapist's sudden absence has unconsciously triggered a repetition from early infancy. Perhaps there had been an actual and sudden maternal absence for Layla and then, as now, there were no words to communicate the sense of nothingness and the terror of annihilation. Winnicott, a paediatrician and psychoanalyst and whom I quote at the beginning of this paper, once had written of an infant's experience of abandonment and terror, as moments of 'unthinkable anxieties, of going to pieces, falling forever, having no relation to the body, no orientation, and no means to communicate.'

Despite however, the team's continuing attempts to raise the issue of the therapist's sudden absence, and her replacement with a new residential therapist, Layla refused to consider it as having a significance. Within the team meetings, she seemed compliant but I observed an increasing sterility in her responses to the team leader's interpretations. On one particular day, following a serious and disturbing row between Layla and another guest, Layla runs out in the street. This is followed by the sound of glass breaking. I immediately go out to find her, but she has disappeared.

Eventually she returns. The team leader reminds her that she is on a Probation Order and that her behaviour is up against the limits. All she can admit to is feeling 'a little angry', but that she also feels numb and frightened. In her session, she paces up and down the consulting room. It is as if she has the potential power and aggression of a caged animal. She is offered a fourth session which she accepts, but before this takes place, she again cuts and burns herself.

In trying to understand her, I remind myself that the rage and hatred she shows towards herself and others, is only part of her psyche. She is also a young woman who can be vulnerable, childlike, and regressed, as on the occasions she has attended sessions bare foot, or carrying a teddy bear. Her persona is that of both the abuser and the abused and she has the capacity to switch from one state of mind to the other. The abuser is represented by her thick, heavy, unfeminine boots, used for kicking cars, for 'breaking and entering', for 'putting the boot in'. Carrying the teddy bear, when she feels little and like the small teddy bear, she needs looking after, then there was no need to cut. She was open to being cared for with words, her feeling were out there, in the room and not 'cut off.'

Layla had told me she wanted to be tough and had fought hard to be seen as tough. Another time she had asked that I didn't see her as tough as she was actually a 'softie' underneath. She also mentioned in passing that she did 'photographic modelling' and that her mother had bought her a long, blond wig for these occasions. She laughed as she said this, but I was curious as to her mother's intentions and I was also intrigued that what Layla told me, put in my mind an image of the exaggerated 'fetishism' of a drag queen.

In my continuing search to understand Layla, I found Kaplan's research helpful.[34] She had found in her therapeutic work with women who cut, the possibility of a very early maternal failure and she writes poignantly of the perversity of the 'cutter' where 'the razor is experienced as a trusted caregiver, the skin the child who is waiting to be cared for and given relief.' Layla's preoccupation with being hugged and her sensitivity towards empty containers, was similarly observed in Kaplan's psychotherapeutic work.

She writes, 'During adolescence they are possessed by a need to define and protect the boundaries of their bodies … for the self-cutter, emotions like sadness, anger, joy and love are thought of as demonic substances that could leak out of the body to cover the world, if it were not contained and controlled' (p. 382).

Kaplan also indicated a possible link between this maternal failure, the development of the woman's sexuality and cutting. Given Layla's vague and guarded references to her fears of being alone at night, a male smell, and her avoidance of speaking of her childhood it had already occurred to the team to wonder if she had been subjected to sexual abuse although we had never found the right moment to raise this with her. She also confided in me, she had worked in a 'sleaze club' and had 'entertained' men by boxing bare-chested.

Several days later Layla's sister rang and asked Layla for a telephone number. Layla refused to give us any further information but the call profoundly disturbed her. She cried bitterly in her session,

---

34 Louise J. Kaplan, *Female Perversions: The Temptations of Emma Bovary.*. Penguin, 1993 [1991].

and asked why people carried on living. She said she'd planned to visit me in the night but instead she'd fallen asleep and dreamt she was poisoning her father with strychnine. Instead she had taken it. My comment that the dream indicated a wish to murder her father, but instead murdered herself, touched some deeply held emotion within her. For twenty minutes she writhed, covered her head, and rocked from one foot to the other, saying she didn't know what to do, and she couldn't think. The disturbance stopped as suddenly as it had started.

The following week, Layla had asked if we could spend our hour together in the pub just down the road from the Crisis Centre. Before we went, I left my bag on a chair in the kitchen to speak to a colleague, but when I returned I could see by Layla's face she had gone through the bag. I said nothing until we got to the pub and sitting down side by side, I ordered our drinks.

Then I said, 'Layla, I think you may have gone through my bag so I'm wondering why and what you were looking for?'

She looked uncomfortable, and was silent initially, then she said 'I want to get into your mind'.

'But it's your mind, not mine, we need to understand.'

'I know you've got two boys, I want to know more about you, and about them, how old are they, and what are their names.'

These questions made me feel uncomfortable and wary. I said, 'Let's talk about you, and your sister. That's more important. What's going on?'

Layla was sitting in a crouching position, her arms wrapped around her legs, her head on her knees.

'She's gone to Ireland.' She said, 'I've been talking to Susie about you, and she agrees with me that you never give a hug freely. You're lying when you say you do.'

I tried to make a link with her need for a hug and to feel held and cared for, but she said 'No matter how many I get, they'll never be enough. I want a permanent hug.'

Suddenly, she leant over, reached for her pint glass half full of coke, and brought it down with force on the round pub table. It smashed into fragments. I froze with fear. An image flashed through my head. She could use one of the pieces of glass to cut my face.

I heard myself say, 'We need to get back.'

I was half aware that the woman behind the bar, had walked over with a dustpan and brush and silently cleared away the shards of glass. We stood up, silently left the pub to walk back to the Centre. Shocked, I could say nothing.

We walked back. My lack of anger enraged Layla even more. She shouted out, 'Why don't you get angry?' and smashed her boot into the side of a car. I was aware in those moments, only of my fear and of her rage, and later back in the Crisis Centre, reflected this was a familiar dynamic. I held the fear and she expressed her anger. It had been a perfect enactment of her persona and the split within herself.

This marked a turning point in our relationship and of her time in the Crisis Centre. I was wary about spending time with her outside the house, and although we continued to spend time together inside, Layla turned away from me and was difficult to engage in any conversation. I, on the other hand was now in touch with my hatred for her, in the way Winnicott had observed and which I now knew at a very deep level within myself. I brought this up in my supervision and was reassured in supervision, this would be temporary.

Meanwhile discussions within the Crisis Centre team had also reached the conclusion, that extending her stay would not be possible. Layla was profoundly disappointed and her feelings of hatred and anger intensified. She threatened she would refuse to leave, and would sleep outside until she was taken in. She said she was planning to throw a brick through the windows of the local police station, the idea again indicating her need for containment.

Even worse, were the vicious attacks on her body. Her bedroom was like a rubbish tip, filled with empty lager cans, lighters, razor blades and general rubbish. Layla said she liked it like this because it was 'her personality', but when I commented perhaps her room represented her own self-hatred, her inner despair and impotence, she surprisingly accepted this interpretation.

In my supervision, I continued to very much want to understand Layla. Even so, I questioned whether she was capable of being helped and whether it was inevitable her drive to destroy what was good. My supervisor pointed out that the early work with the male team leader had represented to her a good parental, caring couple, as evidenced by the times when Layla came to the sessions barefoot, without her boots, and with her teddy bear. However this 'holding environment', which could be seen as a virtual pre-oedipal experience, came to an abrupt end with the sudden disappearance of the resident therapist and her eventual replacement. Here reality had intruded into our work. It meant Layla was confronted, before she was ready, with the loss of the oedipal triangle.

Somehow the team had repeated a trauma that was unbearably familiar to Layla; that of loss, sudden change and annihilating disappointment. The boundaries we had hoped to establish, had not been secure. Worse, we had unwittingly provided a space with no boundaries, which meant Layla had been invaded by the past uncertainties, experiences, events. The containment she had most wanted, a secure 'holding environment' the 'permanent hug' for her had existed, but then was taken away.

Days before she was due to leave, something about Layla's manner raised our suspicions. The residential therapist asked Layla if she had again cut herself. In response, Layla pulled back her tee shirt to reveal horrific, burning and slashing injuries. It looked almost as if she had tried to hack off her arm. As she did this, she looked me fully in the eye and said, 'I told you.' I felt I would faint with horror. How could she do this to herself? How could she have survived such pain? Her face remained hard and empty, determinedly oblivious to the horror of her actions and its effect on ourselves.

How can her behaviour be understood? Layla had been a popular member of the Crisis Centre. She had attended all the team meetings, she contributed to other meetings, and she took her turn to cook for the other guests. But her behaviour was becoming more extreme and perverse. Layla was one of a group at the Crisis Centre, all of whom in varying degrees of seriousness, cut or burned themselves. Layla's attack reigned supreme amongst them, and those of us working in the Crisis Centre, as non-cutters and non-burners, were gradually turned into spectators.

We had become virtual masochistic witnesses to their sadism. But this position could be reversed. We could also be virtually sadistic as we observed their masochistic self-inflicted injuries. In such actions, lies an unspoken accusation, 'Look what you've done to me. You've made me do this to myself. Now look after me.' This perverse relationship between her need to be understood and cared for was in total opposition to her drive to destroy. Layla lived out this split, between masochism and sadism, between body and mind. She used her body as a passive victim, her mind as an active agent. The moment she had decided to attack herself and took the flame or the knife to her flesh, the body's autonomic system took over.

Endorphin was released, a powerful, tranquillising morphine substance. Then she could say, 'Now I feel better, more relaxed' and as Kaplan had observed and interpreted, 'the razor is experienced as a trusted caregiver, the skin the child who is waiting to be cared for and given relief.'

It was not until the evening she left that Layla allowed herself to acknowledge my concern for her. She had asked me once whether I thought she would ever get better and the card I had chosen for her, showed a young woman jumping up and down, with the words, 'never give up'. She seemed visibly moved and later sent me a letter. She thanked me for all the time I spent with her, for my interest, and apologised for the times she refused to talk to me. She said it was all due to what was in her head, which she now knew this was not real.

A month later she came for her follow-up session. I was saddened by her appearance. She was heavily sedated, looked pale and uncared for, and she said she hadn't eaten for three days. I spontaneously asked if she would like to come out for a coffee. She brightened up and as we slowly walked to a café, she asked if I thought she would ever feel safe.

I said, 'Yes, but change takes time and you need to give yourself that time. But one day, you'll wake up and you'll notice that you feel just a little better, and gradually that feeling will grow and strengthen.'

Layla was eventually admitted to an NHS Psychotherapy Unit as an inpatient. The next time I saw her she looked physically well and her skin was blooming. She hugged me and said this would have to be the last time she would see me. I was well aware then as I am now, how much that, despite her violence, her hatred and her perverse self-mutilation, I cared deeply about her. Although her aggression had come close to destroying my concern, somehow, with help, I had held onto the feeling that she was also a vulnerable and fragile young woman and that she was desperate for my acceptance and understanding.

Could our work be considered as having helped her? Working with such deep levels of disturbance takes time and enormous reservoirs of patience and hope. Not only does the therapist need first-class supervision but also needs the necessary commitment and belief in the therapeutic process, because the demands on the psyche can feel punishing.

When I began training, an Arbours therapist had once said to me, patients express a range of desires, disappointments, and confusions, some of which are unacceptable and quite crazy. But to understand them and make sense of them, the therapist must also be prepared to reflect on them. She must know them within herself, because without this self-knowledge which she may need to communicate, the patient will feel isolated and alone.

In other words, a patient and therapist are involved in a mutual relationship of self-discovery. This 'mutual relationship' was described by Winnicott as a 'transitional space' in that it is neither wholly of the inner or of the outer world, but part of both. The work we began at Arbours with Layla was the beginning of that process but it seemed just enough for her to want to continue her journey.

Observing and Interpreting

'The language of the film is the language of the unconscious. For that moment in time, it becomes the reality. The opening scene indicates that possibility. Another imagined world is entered and in this lies a potential to observe and reflect on the excitement, horror, love, violence, or confusion of another life. The experience of watching a film holds therefore a complex paradox. It is as if real, but remains a phantasy.'

— CHAPTER 20 —

Interpretations: the psychic power of narrative nonfiction

Narrative nonfiction has a long history although it has not always been identified in this way. Historically it has given a certain freedom, if not power to the non-fiction writer, as for example, Freud's case histories, many of which have since been collected together in separate volumes. Using this method, Freud's innovatory thinking on the causes of the emotionally troubled, enabled him to write persuasively about the various factors in a patient's life which contributed to their state of mind. We know of these patients through Freud's own interpretation. We see them through his eyes. He has become the virtual stage director of their problematic lives.

Freud as interpreter thus stands between his patient and ourselves, yet by the time we come to read his account, it is, at least, 'third hand'. This being, despite Freud's advocacy and belief in his own ability to listen with evenly suspended attention, surely an impossible ideal. In any narrative, either consciously or unconsciously, particular interpretations are chosen. The originating words belong to the narrator, but their meaning is, incidentally, likely to change with each retelling and the reader's own interpretation.

Donald P. Spence, a psychiatrist, an analyst, and an academic further developed this view. He wrote that Freud's theories which developed from his work with particular patients, and then became written up as case histories can be understood as a metaphor. And the ultimate understanding of any one of these, depends, in the final analysis on interpretations. In other words, they tell a story; they are more philosophical, more hermeneutic than scientific.[35]

But whether an account of a life is acceptable or not, is, to put it simply, dependent on the reader, or the spectator's own frame of reference and whether that is shared or even congruent with the original narrator. At its most basic, there are two ways of telling a story: the factual, as in a scientific paper or a police report. Here there is close attention to facts, what happened and when, and a comparative search for similarities with a given perspective. Ambiguities and language which invite differences between understanding and interpretation are seen as unhelpful. The aim is for clarity and simplicity. Metaphors and symbols are similarly excluded, for reasons of factual consistency.

The second approach can be found in what has been called 'narrative nonfiction' as in this book, or for a different example, Parnell's literary docu-memoir of the 'Forgotten Australians'. Having set out the personal factors which motivated her, the author explicitly situates herself in her writing. She observed that unlike the novelist, narrative non-fiction writing is not wholly dependent on imagination or memory, but derives from the writer having immersed herself into the life of another. This depends upon as she points out, a 'creative empathy' or an 'intuitive understanding'.[36] The writer's own words therefore become the tools in which an actual experience or thought, that is, the essential truth, is mediated and transformed into a narrative.

---

35 Donald P. Spence, *The Freudian Metaphor: Toward Paradigm Change in Psychoanalysis*. W. W. Norton & Co, 1987.
36 Jo Parnell. 'Literary (Creative Nonfiction) Docu-Memoir: A Different Way of Writing a Life Authors', *European Journal of Life Writing* Vol. 3, 2014.

Parnell points to her own personal identification with the lives of abandoned and neglected children in Australia. Their story is her story and it is her own history which gives her account both its power and authenticity. By empathically including herself in their narrative and by writing of her own traumatic childhood, the book is 'framed', and therefore justified by her own experiences which parallel those she writes of.

This form of writing is therefore neither purely factual or purely fictional, since the writer has become part of the analytic narrative. There has been no hypothesis, no collection of data to test a hypothesis since the writer is both the agent and interpreter, situating themselves dynamically somewhere between either role or with both. This perspective can be understood as profoundly political, since the process of interpretation comes from within, as the writer relates and identifies with the experiences of the other. The approach echoes the immediacy and the power of the feminist movement in the sixties and seventies, 'The Personal is Political'. It is also relevant today. It can be argued why some books and films may resonate on a very personal level with some readers and viewers, but not others.

For these same reasons, this memoir *Talk Therapy* includes an account of my own difficult childhood. Written from memory, it is in the style of narrative nonfiction. It documents the experience of myself as a five-year-old living for three months on a Children's Accident Ward and the family experiences which followed. In line with this experience, the writing and style is intentionally different from the rest of the memoir.

It is personal and a narrative. It communicates what was specific to myself; the isolation, the loneliness, the silence, the fear, the loss of trust in the adult world; all states of mind I later saw in certain patients even though derived from a different history. The writing is therefore authentic, powerful and angry, the style spare, and in places, some might see my account as unjustifiably critical, but some may not. These were my experiences which ultimately laid the foundations for my later training and work as a therapist with the Arbours Association. In this, the authority of the 'received view' which is to say, those with the power to define what is acceptable, is challenged. One has only to reflect on the uproar by the monarchists, the tabloid journalists, and the paparazzi as a response to Prince Harry's autobiography, *Spare*.

Writing in this way is not without some difficulties. It stirs things up. Life isn't quite as predictable and reassuring as some expect, hope, and desire. Within a dialogue of a therapeutic session, interpretations give meaning and power to the narrative of the patient. A connection is made between the therapist and the patient and the two aspects of a patient's psyche; one is overt and known, the other ephemeral and intangible. While sometimes seeming to have little connection with the original story or explanation which may have brought the patient to the therapist, such interpretations relate to a symbol, a metaphor, an allegory, a dream, a narrative, a repetition, a joke; any, or all, may be part of the patient's narrative.

The origins to this form of narrative lie in the unconscious, and once understood give further emotional depth to understanding the patient's story. The role of the therapist is to decode the story and present it to the patient in such a way that it's useful within the total analytic process. And although many forms of popular communication such as poetry, music, and novels are popular for communicating an unknown, films also have a long and impressive history of representing states of mind, hence their potential iconic status. They also have particular points of view, derived from the technology of a filmic frame of reference.

— CHAPTER 21 —

Film as Clinical Narrative: when the personal becomes political

If we think of the lens of a camera as representing the human eye, it is through the camera's 'eye' that the imagination of the viewer is initially engaged. In the opening scenes of a film, the reality of the everyday with its expectations of time and space becomes abandoned. The spectator now cocooned in the dark shared space of a cinema, and shielded from the reality of everyday life, can, according to the nature of the film, experience a range of emotions. Oblivious to the outside world, the spectator becomes absorbed in the presentation of another world, thus paralleling the intensity of a child at play.

Hence, the language of the film is the language of the unconscious. For that moment in time, it becomes the reality. The opening scene indicates that possibility. Another imagined world is entered and in this lies a potential to observe the excitement, horror, love, violence, or confusion of another life. The experience of watching a film holds therefore a complex paradox. It is as if real, but remains a phantasy.

Music, also as a fundamental subliminal communication is essential in contributing to the atmosphere of a film. Written specifically to accompany the narrative, the score written by a film composer, consists of a number of cues. These are timed to enhance the drama and emotional impact of particular scenes. For example, American swing was an essential element to the dance films of Fred Astaire and Ginger Rogers (*Swing Time,* 1936) While Ennio Morricone's sublime musical compositions inspired by the sweeping harsh beauty of the American West, with its never-ending struggle between good and evil incorporated the cruelty of conflict between the settlers and the indigenous population (*Once Upon a Time in the West,* 1968). In contrast to this evocation of time and place, the solitary, melancholic tones of the jazz saxophone, have become forever associated with the dark side of American city life in 'film noir' (Sweet Smell of Success, 1957).

Yet underlying much of the storytelling success of the Hollywood studios lies the significant influence of Freudian theory. In 1909 Freud had been invited to lecture at the University of Massachusetts. His theories of the unconscious were already well established in Europe but this trip was the only one he ever made to the States. He brought with him two colleagues, Sándor Ferenczi and Carl Jung, equally well known for their creative adaptations of Freudian theory. Freud reportedly delivered his five lectures in German and without notes. These made a deep impression on the audience, and his approach to analysing neurosis and psychoses became increasingly significant in the developing academic and cultural life of twentieth century America.

In 1999 Glen Gabbard, an American psychoanalyst together with his brother, Krin Gabbard, a teacher of film and cultural studies, and the author of several books on jazz, released the second edition of their book, *Psychiatry and the Cinema*.[37] They note firstly, the public's confusion between psychiatry, psychotherapy and psychology; a confusion also prevalent in the UK. Their book

---

37 Glen O. Gabbard and Krin Gabbard, *Psychiatry and the Cinema*. American Psychiatric Association Publishing, 1999.

also references 450 films which depict psychiatry or psychiatrists and a preoccupation with how psychiatrists and analytic theory are represented.

Films linked for example, with the Lacanian concept of the mirror (*Breaking the Waves,* 1996), Oedipal theory (*Casablanca*, 1942) or narcissism (Scorsese's *The King of Comedy*, 1982) as well as in many of Woody Allen's films. But above them all, the director, Hitchcock, reigned supreme. His ability and awareness of the anarchic and destructive force of the unconscious was woven into the narrative of many of his films. (*Psycho* 1960, *Marnie* 1964, *Rear Window* 1954, *The Birds*, 1963). They make for uncomfortable viewing but can be 'read' as filmic case studies of disturbance and perversity.

Bearing these points in mind, what follows is a discussion and an analysis of three films. Chosen because of their 'essential truth', the artistry in telling a story and the observation of character as a reflection of an historical moment in time, once seen, it is likely they remain indelibly fixed in the viewers' mind. In these films, subtle references as to why a character behaves in particular ways is explored through the development of their relationships, dialogue and flashbacks, and provide some understanding of the origins and the subsequent trajectory of psychic conflict and disturbance. They are therefore of particular interest within the context of this memoir, (as opposed to the analysis by a film student) since they are open to an analytic discussion of meaning.

In terms of the expression of art's contribution to understanding psychological disturbance, they are the filmic equivalent of Steinbeck's compassionate anger in *The Grapes of Wrath* (1939), of Jane Austin's acerbic observations in *Pride and Prejudice* (1813), of Dylan Thomas' lyricism of childhood in the poem *Fern Hill* (1945), of Miles Davis' horn with its staccato solitary opening in *So What* (1959). In other words, the main characters 'act out' some universal conflicts of life, but instead of being related in the privacy of a therapeutic session, they are framed within a film's narrative. The private has become public. The context, political.

Andrea Sabbadini, a London based psychoanalyst known for his extensive knowledge and interest in film writes in his monograph, *Moving Images*, of the many thematic affinities between cinema and psychoanalysis. He notes the characters on screen may remind us of our own psychoanalytic work. His discussions on film are intricate and analytically informed and organised round films which share a number of psychoanalytic themes, such as childhood, adolescence, love, or voyeurism.[38]

By way of comparison, here the following three films were chosen on the basis of a single issue problematic. During the process of observing how a film's narrative unfolded, all three in different ways represent therapeutically relevant issues which may confront the therapist at some point in their work:[39]

Muriel's Wedding: *Parental Failure, Female Friendship and the Cultural Significance of Weddings;*

The Night Porter: *The Perverse Attraction of the 'Bad Object';*

Last Year at Marienbad: *The Allure of the Dream. The Uncertainty of Memory. The Dread of Forgetting.*

---

38 Andrea Sabbadini, *Moving Images: Psychoanalytic Reflections on Film*. Routledge, 2014.
39 Accounts of all three films were earlier written in a different form and with different titles. Published in two analytic journals, they have been abbreviated and rewritten for this book.

— CHAPTER 22 —

Muriel's Wedding: parental failure, female friendship and the cultural significance of weddings

'Life is a tragedy for those who feel and a comedy for those who think', so wrote Jean de la Bruyère, the French seventeenth century philosopher and satirist. Others have observed the thin line dividing both states of mind. But here we are 'privileged' to have both. The Australian film, *Muriel's Wedding* is about the developing friendship between two women. It begins in an imaginary small town, called Porpoise Spit, which is followed by the friends' move to Sydney. Although *Muriel's Wedding* is usually understood as a comedy, the film is deeper than this, since humour and tragedy are integrally interwoven throughout the film.

Released in 1994 it quickly became a worldwide success. Written by P J Hogan, with music by Abba, the two main protagonists were played by Toni Collette as Muriel and Rachel Griffiths as Rhonda. The music and lyrics of Abba's 'Dancing Queen' in particular is significant, since it is emblematic of Muriel's fantasies to be beautiful and desired. It is her 'go to' song when she is particularly depressed. Hogan thus appropriates the words and music of Abba to highlight Muriel's fascination with weddings. As a bride, she phantasies, only thus will she overcome her depression and envied for her beauty and attractiveness.

The film's narrative is as follows. Muriel sees herself as a deeply unattractive and overweight female. She is an outsider both within her family and her peer group. Her mother is deeply depressed and drifts through life in a trance. Despite her husband's constant denigration and aggression (for example, he barely conceals his affair which he conducts under her nose, and the contempt with which he views his children), she remains apparently oblivious, untouched and untroubled by any deep emotion.

Muriel's response to this is to construct an elaborate phantasy, one to which she compulsively turns when facing difficulties. The phantasy is that she will one day become a bride. Insofar as the narrative seems to replicate the story of Cinderella, Hogan ultimately gives a different 'take' on the story. He replaces the 'prince' with an alternative possibility; that of Muriel's relationship with a female friend who transforms Muriel's inner world.

From the start of the film, Muriel is shown as scapegoated by her family, her father, and the circle of totally obnoxious friends all of whom without conscience use her as the recipient of their sadistic thoughts and feelings about themselves and the world. Such scenes put in mind the work of Harold Searles (see Chapter 11) who identified the underlying destructiveness of such verbal transactions in his paper, 'The Effort to Drive the Other Person Crazy.'[40]

Although the film initially, it seems, is based on the story of Cinderella, whereby a handsome, rich prince rescues her from a life of persecuting drudgery, instead the film presents an alternative resolution. It depicts how Muriel's unsatisfactory relationship with

---

40 Harold Searles, 'The Effort to Drive the Other Person Crazy: An Element in the Aetiology and Psychotherapy of Schizophrenia', *British Journal of Medical Psychology*, Vol 32(1): 1–18, 1959.

her mother is worked through via the development of her friendship with Rhonda.

Rhonda is seemingly everything Muriel would like to be. She is attractive, aggressive, self-confident and highly sexual. She is also able to identify with Muriel's unhappiness but deals with it in a different way. She tells Muriel to 'stick around' because she is 'wicked'. The two friends leave their small home town of Porpoise Spit to live in Sydney where, under Rhonda's influence, and away from the negative experience of her family and peer group. Muriel begins to develop her self-confidence, enjoy life, and explore her sexuality and interest in men. She also changes her name to Marial which represents her new-found happiness via her friendship with Rhonda. At the same time she has simultaneously rejected the family name of Muriel with its memories of persecution and psychological abuse.

This idyllic state of affairs is short-lived. Following one of Rhonda's excitable sexual and humorous adventures with two men, Rhonda loses the sensation in her legs. This is subsequently diagnosed as cancer of the spine. Paradoxically at this point it seems that despite the overall feminist perspective in the film, the moral here or it is so implied, is that if women fail to conform to the stereotypical notion of sexual abstinence, then they are punished. For example, Rhonda asks the doctor following the diagnosis, 'It's nothing to do with too much sex, is it?'

Yet Hogan is accurately depicting many women's anxieties. It is not uncommon for women to perceive, for example, unwanted pregnancies, contracting herpes, or rape, as punishment for sexual activity.

But it is at the point that Rhonda is diagnosed with a potentially terminal cancer, that Muriel compulsively returns to her fantasy of the wedding and finding her 'prince'. In symbolic terms Muriel is now faced with the terrifying prospect of maternal abandonment through the death of her friend This thought is unbearable and she feels compelled to act out her phantasy. She answers an advertisement for an Australian woman to marry a South African swimmer to enable him to stay in the country.

The application is successful and Muriel's obsession with weddings becomes more and more evident, to the point of a major rift developing between the two friends. Shortly before Rhonda confronts her, a scene in the film shows Muriel trying on wedding dresses. The shop assistant asks her whether her mother will be coming in to see the dress. Muriel replies, 'No, she's in hospital. She has a tumour.'

Whether Muriel is ultimately aware or not of her phantasy that she symbolically perceives Rhonda as her mother, her answer clearly identifies the importance of Rhonda for Muriel. But this a dyadic relationship. Both are unconsciously working through their parallel needs through the other. Muriel's terror at losing Rhonda is also experienced by Rhonda. If Muriel marries, Rhonda will lose her, because Muriel also represents an idealised mother for Rhonda, hence their subsequent passionate conflict. Each feels betrayed by the other.

One might hypothesise that the possible loss of Rhonda is a repetition for Muriel of earlier experiences with her emotionally dead mother. Her frantic search for the perfect wedding dress leads to the film's first dénouement, whereby Rhonda, now in a wheelchair and, having tracked Muriel down, angrily confronts her in the bridal dress shop. Muriel cries out in a self-revelatory moment, 'If I get married, it means I can change. I can become a new person … If someone wants to marry me. I'm not her any more. I'm me … I'm fat and useless, and I'm not going back to be her. Why can't I be the one?' 'The one' is the fantasised, desired and beautiful 'princess'.

The Cultural and Psychological Significance of Weddings

Muriel's obsession with weddings demonstrates their significance to her inner world. But sociologically, all weddings are a 'spectacle' since wherever they take place, they are invested with powerful (but different) meanings. Stephanie Harzewski, for example, notes how weddings in Western society take place within an arena where politics, the economy and culture interact with the personal i.e. psychology and the unconscious. She writes that lavish weddings enable the couple to project a powerful image of social prestige, and notes how they contribute to maintaining a specific female role in Western Society. She also makes an important observation, that weddings have become dissociated from what follows; marriage. She writes, 'In varying degrees, brides across the globe are increasingly appropriating the interdependent elements of fantasy, magic and romantic love permeating Western popular culture and Hollywood films.'[41]

These are all important points since they relate to the contemporary cultural context in which women find themselves in the West, but in analysing *Muriel's Wedding* other observations can be made. Firstly, those relating to the unconscious aspects of Muriel's wedding enactment, and secondly, how the resolution of her dilemmas is ultimately worked through within the film's narrative.

Marrying the swimmer enables Muriel to act out her fantasy of becoming a bride. A scene shows her radiant before the assembled congregation. One might hypothesise that in her imagination she casts herself as both performer and spectator. She is now, to paraphrase one of her favourite Abba songs in the film, 'the dancing queen, having the time of her life' and the congregation in the church are to 'watch that girl, the dancing queen'. She processes down the central aisle to the music of another Abba tune, 'I do, I do, I do'. But within the humour of the scene, the choice of music, the shocked faces of the congregation, the triumph over the spiteful friends (the stepsisters) now cast in a subordinate role as bridesmaids, there begins a necessary disillusion. Muriel begins the process of a profound internal shift.

Following the wedding she perceives the painful discontinuity between fantasy and reality. Her new husband barely conceals his contempt for her. He tells her he has no love for her. It is a marriage

---

41 Stephanie Harzewski, 'Consuming Heteroscripts: The Modern Wedding in the American Imaginary', *Iowa Journal of Cultural Studies* 4, Spring 2004.

of convenience, which, she now understands is as exploitative as that of her own choices; the reality of marriage differs from the fantasy of a wedding.

But there are other changes. Her mother, passive and suffering, finds herself excluded from the wedding and Muriel's life. Her husband has left her and her remaining children treat her with arrogant indifference. She is an outsider, a role once held by Muriel. But, unlike Muriel, she has no capacity to fantasise, a defence which though a form of dissociation can be seen as self-protective. She finds it unbearable, and tragically commits suicide.

In a final scene, Muriel is shown standing with her father contemplating the backyard of her home where her mother, prior to her suicide, had set fire to the garden. It is a scene of utter devastation. It is her mother's only act of protest, showing her internal desolation shortly before she destroyed herself. Muriel no longer retreats to a fantasy of weddings, but is now thoughtful and sad. Her father faces life without his wife. and turning to Muriel he pressurises her to stay and look after the family. It is a crucial moment. To stay would be to identify with the role of her mother, and to repeat a pattern. Muriel declines. She says, 'You owe us, Dad.'

The Importance of Disillusionment to Psychic Growth

Muriel has become conscious to the reality of alternative ways of how she might live. She makes her choice. She fetches Rhonda from the clutches of her mother and the 'ugly sisters' and the two return to Sydney. As they drive away Rhonda throws a final insult at the 'ugly sisters'. As she and Muriel leave in a cab (not the glass coach), she shouts, 'What a bunch of cocksuckers!' Though expressed in the language of the street, and a reference to earlier scenes of fellatio, this too can be interpreted analytically. It shows their joint contempt for the women's type of relationship with men.

Viewed from this perspective, how might Muriel's wedding finally be understood? The idea of the 'wedding' is the heart of the film and is a visual representation of her fantasy. The experience epitomises for Muriel the gratification of all she desires, but it is also a manic fantasy. In Winnicott's classic paper on the manic defence, he writes of it thus: 'Fantasy is part of the individual's effort to deal with inner reality. It can be said that fantasy and daydreams are omnipotent manipulations of external reality.'[42]

Muriel's obsession with weddings was a defence against her depression and her dread of the deadness of the internalised primary object, her mother. As Winnicott commented, when we are manic-defensive we are least likely to feel depressed, because we feel elated, happy, busy, excited etc.[43] He makes a further important observation, he points to the difference between a phantasy and that of imagining. He sees the former as absorbing energy, but not contributing to either living or dreaming. It is a form of dissociation.[44]

The end of the film shows Muriel has risen above her wedding phantasy. By refusing her father's emotional pressures to take her mother's place within the family, she makes her choice. She 'sticks' around for and with Rhonda, and this decision enables her, and shows us, the beginning of her own journey to finding herself.

---

42 Donald W. Winnicott, 'The Manic Defence', in *Through Paediatrics to Psychoanalysis*. Karnac Books, 1992.
43 Ibid, p. 132.
44 Donald W. Winnicott, 'Reparation in Respect of Mother's Organized Defence Against Depression, in *Through Paediatrics to Psychoanalysis*. Karnac Books, 1992.

— CHAPTER 23 —

The Night Porter: the perverse attraction of the 'Bad Object'

No one who sees the film *The Night Porter* (1974) will leave the cinema without feeling disturbed and shocked. Its narrative is nightmarish. Its action and characterisation are not merely those of a bad dream, its impact is derived from the film's ability to recreate a reality; that of the claustrophobic perversity of sadomasochism. But it is also essential to recognise its underlying political critique; it is a metaphor for the breakdown of a society.

The Night Porter was written and directed by the Italian woman director Liliana Cavani. It is regarded as her masterpiece. It is hauntingly disturbing. Shot in the style of 'film noir', it traces the deterioration of a sexually sadistic relationship between Lucia, a young Jewish woman, played by the coldly beautiful Charlotte Rampling and Max, a Nazi guard, played by Dirk Bogarde, whom she first encountered in a concentration camp fourteen years previously.

The year is now 1957. Their chance meeting takes place against the brutal, aesthetic formalism of a Viennese Art Deco hotel and the intermittent background music of Mozart's *The Magic Flute*. The film's narrative traces the characters' development of their perverse obsession with each other and their gradual psychological deterioration. The final scenes show how, within the confines of a locked apartment, they recreate the psychotic claustrophobia of the concentration camp.

From the viewpoint of analytic theory it is as I shall discuss, a traumatic re-enactment of an internalised object relation.[45] Tragically and inexorably, death becomes their only means of escape. The film is memorable because it unrelentingly focuses on their doomed psychological relationship. To illustrate this, Cavani makes full and frequent use of the flashback, thus indicating to the spectator that the two protagonists are possessed by their history.

For example, an early scene in the film shows a line of naked prisoners in the concentration camp. Max holds a camera attached to a powerful arc light, picks out, and then shoots with a brilliant light the face and naked body of Lucia. We see her through his eyes and, in a reverse shot, we see him through her eyes. The camera represents both the power of a gun and of the phallus, symbolising the prescient colonisation of her body and mind. Both are to become possessed by the other.

The film begins with a low light shot. It is raining and Max is seen walking across a square, his face hidden behind an umbrella. He walks into the hotel where he is employed as the night porter. His latent cruelty quickly becomes apparent. He uses a perverse and subtle power to subjugate the other, whether male and female. He denies one of the guests, a countess, water with which to swallow her medication, and cruelly summons a gigolo to satisfy her sexual desires. Every gesture, every facial expression expresses hatred and contempt. Into this hotel arrives Lucia with her husband, conductor of the opera, *The Magic Flute*.

The ambience of the surroundings suggests culture and refinement, a world away from the Nazi concentration camp. Lucia

---

45 See https://www.encyclopedia.com/psychology/
dictionaries-thesauruses-pictures-and-press-releases/internal-object

is poised and sophisticated; Max epitomises an arrogant servility. Their recognition of each other is immediate, mutual, disturbing. Both experience flashbacks. We see in one, the naked Lucia pursued by Max who fires at her as she runs and attempts to hide from him in a filthy bathroom in the concentration camp.

In a later scene which takes place at the opera house, Lucia sits in front of Max. She feels compelled to glance at him over her shoulder. In this action she visualises the degradation of the concentration camp, re-experiencing again how Max used his power to control, torment and humiliate her. We see her chained and, in a rare close-up, Max slowly and deliberately inserting his two fingers into her mouth, simulating sexual intercourse, this representing the destructive power of the gun and its association with the phallus. The contrast with the refined symbolism of *The Magic Flute* cannot be greater. It is an inspired image of sadistic eroticism.

Max takes increasing psychological control of her. He cancels the call Lucia books to her husband, and lets himself into her room with his key: this symbolically representing the ease with which he can invade her mind and body. He then psychologically and physically assaults her. A scene of brutal sex follows, where Lucia's covert masochism becomes apparent. It is clear she finds such cruelty, sexually exciting. Whereas, in flashback scenes set in the concentration camp, Lucia is shown as passively enduring Max's abuse, now she has relinquished any resistance. She has become his collaborator and complicit in her abuse. It is a critical scene, indicating the movement away from a life conventionally lived to the decline into perversity.

The film shows them increasingly losing touch with reality. When Max leaves their rented apartment, he imprisons Lucia by chaining her arms and legs. She watches with passive amusement. There is no resistance. It is an enactment of their shared addictive state of mind. In a powerful symbol of her caged madness, a cat showing obvious signs of distress paces the floor and mews pitifully. Like this animal, Lucia crouches under the table, dragging her chains behind her. Deprived of food and social contact, starving and exhausted, their self-care becomes minimal.

They live in squalor. Lucia smashes open a jar of jam which she frantically eats, holding the jam-covered shards of glass millimetres away from her mouth. Even at this late stage they play a sado-masochistic 'game', whereby Max attempts to force the glass into her face. The atmosphere is murderous.

Max is shown then enacting a final act of perversion. He dresses Lucia in the clothes of a young girl, referring to her as his 'little girl'. Although this might relate to Lucia's experiences of sexual abuse as a child, within the film the meaning is obscure, and is a repetition of an earlier scene shown as a flashback from the concentration camp. He then flings open the windows of the apartment, as if to let in the light, but outside it is dark. The action suggests they are to escape, but it is the final scene.

In a low light shot, we see Max wearing the uniform of a Nazi guard. They are shown walking unsteadily together over a bridge. It is dawn, and the urban landscape is cold and devoid of figures. The ending is sudden and brutal. Shots are fired. A member of a Nazi gang who shared their history murders them.

The Role of Complicity in Sadomasochism

How might this enactment be understood? In *The Night Porter* we are given no indication of the protagonists' early history, but we might infer this from clinicians who have worked with patients engaged in explicit and unmitigated sadism within their sexual relationships. Their accounts demonstrate that a shared language, which could hold the possibility of communicating the original trauma, is either corrupted, inaccessible or non-existent, and becomes displaced into forms of bodily acting out.

What is remarkable in the film is, as commented earlier, the lack of dialogue. One possible explanation is that the originating traumatic object relations were experienced at the pre-verbal stage. Since Freud, who observed, 'The ego is first and foremost a bodily ego',[46] many other analytic theoreticians have observed that the early sense of self originates in bodily sensations.

Bick's now classic paper on the psychic role of the skin is also of significance here. She writes that the skin functions as a boundary, but this symbolic function of containing parts of the self is dependent on the introjection of a good external object. Without the experience of a containing object, the infant engages in a frantic search for a light, a voice, a smell, or another sensual object, which momentarily functions to hold the parts of the personality together (Bick 1986). The relevance of this theoretical insight may be appreciated by the scene which occurs midway through the narrative in The Night Porter.

Here Cavani shows in cinematic form how Max and Lucia gradually psychically fragment and collaborate in an act of self-harm. Lucia smashes a glass in the bathroom and lures Max to step on the broken glass, thus cutting his feet. Both see this as exciting. The interaction holds the perversity and contradiction of sadomasochism. It appears that Lucia holds the power. It appears that Max consents to her 'game'. It is 'as if' it is pleasurable and harmless. It enables Lucia to 'care for' and dress his wounds. Here a terrible contradiction is enacted. The film is a metaphor. It represents not only psychological sadism but also the murderous sadism of the Nazi era. Each is a reflection of the other.

A similar dynamic is depicted towards the end of the film, as described earlier. Here Lucia smashes a jar of jam, and Max attempts to force fragments of the glass into her face. Such interactions are sadistic and literal enactments of a breakdown, and the possible repetition of an early experience where there was no containing object. Neither Lucia nor Max can put into words their psychotic anxiety and symbiotic hatred for themselves and the other.

Fairbairn's paper 'The Repression and the Return of Bad Objects … (with Special Reference to the "War Neuroses")'[47] discusses how

---

46 Sigmund Freud 'The Ego and the Id'. Hogarth Press, 1927.
47 W.R.D Fairburn, 'The Repression and the Return of Bad Objects … (with Special Reference to the "War Neuroses")' in *Psychoanalytic Studies of the Personality*, pp. 59-81. Routledge, 1994 [1947].

Freud's original drive-based theory has been transformed. Firstly, by Abraham's inclusion of developmental considerations, and then later by Klein's concept of internalised objects. Fairbairn had argued that Freud's thesis needed recasting, viz. he argued that libidinal 'aims' are of secondary importance to object relating, and that a relationship with the object, and not gratification of impulse, is the ultimate aim.[48] His theory does, it would seem, provide a framework within which to understand sadomasochism.

His work with problem children, victims of an assault, but unable to give an account of their trauma, had perplexed him. He considered the argument that such repression was because the 'the victim of a sexual assault was actuated by guilt over the unexpected gratification of libidinal impulses', but goes on to write he was suspicious and unconvinced by this explanation. What Fairbairn advocates is this; that the revival of a traumatic event represents the relationship with the bad object, and therefore it can 'never be contemplated with equanimity'[49]

He develops his thesis further by considering how the 'bad object' has become internalised, and the consequences of this. Observing the power of the 'bad object', he writes that: 'The child not only internalises his bad objects, because they force themselves upon him and he seeks to control them, but also, and above all, because he *needs them* (my emphasis). If a child's parents are bad objects, he cannot reject them, even if they do not force themselves upon him; for he cannot do without them.'[50]

Hence the difficulty in working with such patients. As Fairbairn says, the patient is 'haunted' by his bad objects. He has internalised and then repressed them, and such a relationship can hardly escape being either sadistic or masochistic. In the same paper he refers to his work with military combatants who experienced a breakdown as a consequence of war. He writes that he has no doubt that a predisposing factor to psychosis was separation-anxiety, and that military conditions exploit 'infantile dependence'.

48 Ibid, pp. 60.
49 Ibid, pp. 63.
50 Ibid, pp. 67.

Elsewhere, he comments that the Nazi regime deliberately cultivated dependence on the State.[51] Under conditions of success, the regime remains a good object. Under conditions of failure, the regime becomes a bad object. As such, the return of the bad object implies a failure of the defence of repression, which now becomes replaced by acute anxiety and dependency[52] Other authors have observed the relationship between State authoritarianism and the sado-masochistic state of mind such as Khan (1989), the critical theorist, Adorno (2005) and George Steiner (1971).[53]

Sadomasochism as a Defence Against Psychic Death

Stoller (1979, 1985, 1986) has devoted a considerable part of his life's work to thinking and writing about how perversion may be understood.[54] Although he notes the ambiguity in the term 'perversion', he describes it in the following way: The desire to hurt, harm, be cruel to, degrade, humiliate someone (including, at levels of lesser awareness, the desire to harm oneself). In the case of perversion, the person to be harmed (besides oneself—but that is often to be unperceived) is one's sex object.[55]

He notes the importance of a 'sexual script' based on secrecy and excitement, the enactment of which attempts to reproduce and repair the original repressed traumas and frustrations. He perceives the unconscious 'contract' between the sadist and the masochist, whereby the masochist gives power to the sadist to play the role of master; the sadist thus becoming the slave to the masochist's desire.

---

51 Ibid. p. 284
52 ibid. pp. 80 et seq.
53 Masud Khan, *Alienation in Perversions*. Karnac Books, 1989; Theodor Adorno, *Minima Moralis: Reflections on a Damaged Life*. Verso, 2005; George Steiner, *In Bluebeard's Castle: Some Notes Towards the Redefinition of Culture*. Faber and Faber, 1971.
54 Robert J. Stoller, *Dynamics of Erotic Life*. Maresfield Library, 1979; Robert J. Stoller, *Observing the Erotic Imagination*. Yale University Press, 1985; Robert J. Stoller, *Perversion: The Erotic Form of Hatred*. Karnac Books, 1986
55 Stoller, 1986, p. 7

Stoller powerfully encapsulates this dynamic in the following statement, 'Masochism is the attack, suffering is my revenge'[56]

In an interesting aside, Stoller notes a recurrent theme in much pornography. The woman is initially represented as cool, superior, uninterested, but is destined to lose control—presumably and stereotypically, this representing and reinforcing, for the reader or the viewer, the potency of the male and the weakness of the woman.

And Khan in 'The Role of Will and Power in Perversions' begins his paper rather strikingly with the phrase: 'There are those that fuck from desire; and those that fuck from intent. The latter are the perverts.'[57] The point he wishes to make is that where there is the exercise of will and power (my emphasis) to achieve an end, then there is perversion. Thus there is a psychic connection between the ideology of authoritarian political beliefs and sadomasochism, as many others have noted.

Each draws on the dehumanisation of the other. This can be counterposed to desire and love, which depends on mutuality and reciprocity for its gratification. Khan further argues that, where two people are engaged in a perverse sexual act, there is a merging of an 'active' and a 'passive' will, which are 'autonomously separate yet symbiotically empathetic'. Thus, 'All perversions account for a symbiotic complicity between two persons, which is both unconscious and empathetic' (ibid. p. 201), and he shares with Stoller the recognition of the original role of intense psychic pain, a trauma, which has become transformed and sexualised into rage and hate. Karen Horney, writing many decades earlier, also considers the argument that masochism is essentially a striving towards the relinquishment of self. She concludes that, although true in some cases, in others it is not apparent. She describes two main tendencies within the masochistic character; one is 'self-minimising', where there are feelings of, and a portrayal of themselves as insignificant, unattractive, stupid and worthless.

---

56   Stoller, 1979, p. 125.
57   Masud Khan, 'The Role of Will and Power in Perversions' in Khan, M. *Alienation in Perversions*. Karnac Books, 1989.

She contrasts this with narcissism. The other is a dependency which is so extreme as to be parasitic. Here there is a craving to the point of insatiability for affection, attention or interest (Horney 1966, p. 252). Clearly, both characteristics of dependency and worthlessness are integral to each other and, given this, it is hardly surprising that such relationships are replete with hostility. Anticipating the later observations of both Stoller and Khan, Horney comments that the hostility of the masochistic type often has a sadistic character.

There is a power in feeling weak and humiliated, and in making others responsible for that suffering. She writes that, although suffering is painful, abandoning one's self may serve as an opiate against pain (ibid, p 275).

All these observations have significance in analysing *The Night Porter*. The director and writer, Cavani, understands very well the dynamics of sadomasochism, which she expresses both through the film's narrative and by her powerful use of visual symbols. For example, she shows Max and Lucia's immediate and unconscious attraction for each other when after many years they unexpectedly meet again in a hotel. A 'look' is exchanged. It passes from one to the other. The scene is unspoken and therefore more powerful for that, since it draws on the viewer's imagination and curiosity.

The film illustrates Khan's observation of the unconscious 'symbiotic complicity'. In another scene just before their deaths, Lucia is filmed, half-lying, half-leaning, her leg bent backwards against a wall in the apartment. It's as if she is a broken doll. It is Cavani's representation of the puppet to which Khan's account of a masochistic female patient refers, 'She became a puppet upon which he actualized his will.'[58]

---

58 Masud Khan, *Alienation in Perversions*, p. 208. Karnac Books, 1989.

— CHAPTER 24 —

Last Year at Marienbad: the allure of dreaming, the uncertainty of memory, the dread of forgetting

If *Muriel's Wedding* is universally seen as both a tragedy and a comedy (although more commonly the latter) and *The Night Porter* as depicting a shocking case of sadomasochism (although not usually as a political metaphor) how can *Last Year at Marienbad* be defined?

The film was released in 1961, its director Alain Resnais, was already known for his films attuned to memories of suffering and loss (*Hiroshima Mon Amour*, 1959). Even so, despite an early recognition that *Last Year at Marienbad* was destined to become iconic, its makers found themselves confronted with contrasting, if not challenging and contradictory reviews. Generally, its beauty and artistry were both appreciated and acknowledged, but its lack of a linear narrative, its repetitions, its overall surrealist obscurity left many perplexed, and furthermore suspicious of its authenticity.

Perceived as 'intellectually pretentious', one reviewer (correctly) observed that whereas many American film releases are rigidly plot driven, in *Marienbad* it was a 'tool for exploration and introspection'. Instead of linear storytelling, he writes that the director, Resnais allows his characters to explore the details of what may be memory or 'just imagination'. Or, more critically another reviewer wrote, that it was a 'bizarre maze of half-recollections and inaccuracies, where words and events are repeated several times in different situations'.

Such contrasting evaluations were intriguing, and having watched the film several times, (and I have to say, found it entrancing) it seemed that the overall narrative could be compared to that of a disturbed and traumatised patient, who in any one session may repeat the telling of apparently the same incident with differences of time and interpretation. This inevitably can lead to confusion within the therapist, which on reflection, was similar to how the film was commonly perceived by those sitting in an audience waiting to be engaged by the film's narrative.

Returning to the comparison with a therapeutic session, it is likely to be unclear to the therapist which parts of the account are factually 'true' i.e. what actually happened. Alternatively, the view might be taken that the original story has been engulfed by another similar narrative, without the narrator's conscious knowledge. However, the authenticity of a session might well depend on the narrator's expression of emotion, which is where the concept of an 'essential truth' is of importance. Therefore to understand this film, it is necessary to travel with the film's overall narrative to understand the purpose of the director's journey.

From the start, I had been aware in watching this film, of its profound affect. Its atmosphere is mesmerising, the characters, dialogue and the narrative dreamlike. This alerted me to the possibility I was the recipient of a powerful projective identification. Therefore, my thoughts seemed to echo those of others who, puzzled by their own responses were unsure whether to take the film seriously, and to wonder whether they were being deceived by Resnais. Was it a profound example of innovatory film-making or merely a pastiche of disconnected experiences?

By following through both my emotional and intellectual responses I came to a conclusion that Resnais' film was indeed deeply authentic. It is about dreaming, and imagining, and the memories and feelings of unrequited desire, of time and place as they play out between the two main characters, called X and A. The power of the film rests on its aesthetic poetry and on Resnais' brilliance in his ability to communicate between reality and states of mind which are in an everyday sense both inaccessible and unknown. His focus is on the minutiae of life, whether experienced by the eye (what something or somebody looks like), the dialogue, whether it makes sense or not, and what 'happens' or hasn't happened, are all aspects which might or might not be part of reality. We just don't know, which is a state of mind profoundly disturbing for many, if not intolerable, since a life lived without apparent order or meaning, necessarily gives rise to a state of 'ontological insecurity'.

The music that accompanies the film is abstract, by which I mean it is not apparently played to express emotion, but to further the powerful feelings of disassociation. It is atonal, harsh, there is a lack of harmony, and with no apparent beginning or end, its style therefore in keeping with X's restless search.

In the opening scene, we hear, but do not see the narrator X: 'I made my way once again' 'where the sounds of footsteps are absorbed', through 'endless corridors' of this 'dismal Baroque hotel.' The rhythm of the speech is slow and relentless in its mode of delivery. The camera pans upwards at the ceiling, and we are given shots of the ornate carvings, chandeliers and mirror reflections. The camera in one long tracking shot focuses down the deserted corridors. The atmosphere is deathly, as with a beautifully preserved but ultimately empty museum. The same narration is repeated several times, with subtle variations, while first X's voice and then the background organ music fades, each taking pre-eminence over the other, expressing the hypnotic and obsessive feelings of the narrator.

The fugue-like structure of X's thoughts seems to indicate a state of mind, a dissociation, a dream-like state, where the external world is symmetrised with his internal world, time and space being negated with the consequent absence of memory. Thus the music and cinematography are symbiotic, each medium consonant with the other.

The film has no chronological narrative and gives no indicators which would enable the viewer to interpret the passage of time, the validity of, or the meaningfulness of its dialogue. Even the protagonists are nameless and are represented by alphabetic symbols. Without such markers of convention, we as spectators are lost. X states he had an affair with A the previous year. A denies this, and the validity of X's claim is never known, and X, albeit subtly, becomes represented as an 'unreliable narrator'. Thus we are destined never to know the 'truth', never to know with certainty whether his mind was held by a phantasy, a longing for A, or whether the film is about a dream, or whether it is actually a dream.

A, who epitomises Parisian chic, and the sinister, cadaverous-looking M, who may or may not be her husband, move within a tightly controlled, choreographed sequence within a vast ornately decorated Baroque hotel. X's narration is notable for its lack of metaphor and for its repetition, with some minor differences, its structure somewhat resembling that of musical counterpoint. 'I was waiting for you … someone who may never come … someone who will separate us, to take you away from me', but A counters: 'This hope no longer has a purpose. This story is already over.'

It is this hopelessness of 'not knowing' portrayed as it is in a poetic form which may indicate that the point of the film, at an unconscious level, is not whether or not an affair took place, but what A might represent for X. The non-chronological narrative makes sense only if we imagine that memory has frozen and time is standing still, just as it might for someone who 'falls' from the experience of who they are, of consistent maternal tenderness and care, and who, experiencing intense anxiety as the consequence of an absent and disappointing object, becomes increasingly desperate, finally withdraws into the comparative safety of an inner world.

Such overwhelming despair forms the origins for what Eleanore Armstrong-Perlman called the 'allure of the bad object'.[59] She observed that, where there is a 'perverse' or an 'addictive' object choice (as A might represent for X), there is a search for a relationship which holds an apparent promise, one which has the potential to restore the lost unity of the self. She goes on to say that this attraction is compulsive, but the object inevitably lacks a reciprocal capacity to love, and that the search is destined to end in rejection. (This is a dynamic which arose between Max and Lucia as earlier discussed in *The Night Porter*).

Dreaming

Freud's model of the unconscious was comprised of five characteristics: condensation, displacement, absence of negation, timelessness, and the confusion of inner fantasy with outer reality. In *Marienbad* all five of these elements may be observed. Resnais has constructed particular scenes designed to create within the viewer similar confusions to the dreamer who in recalling a dream, feels total bemusement as to its meaning.

As for example, in the opening scenes of the film, our attention is drawn fleetingly to a notice attached to a door. It is an advertisement for a play entitled *Rosmer*. Then we are led into an auditorium as if spectators, but watch others spectating whose expressionless faces turn towards an initially unseen stage. Here a grotesquely made-up couple stand so still and silent as to be wax-works. We are thus obliged to experience a Kafkaesque absence of causality, contiguity, and therefore of meaningful action or narration. What confronts us is our own initial experience (watching the film), within another experience (watching the members of the chateau within the film), within another experience (who watch a play), this teleologically looping back to ourselves as spectators.

---

59 Eleanore M. Armstrong-Perlman, 'The Allure of the Bad Object', Journal of the British Association of Psychotherapists, No. 22. https://www.fairbairnresource.co.uk/allure-of-the-bad-object

In most films, a dream is generally perceived conventionally and problematically, since there is a convention of causality and predictable time–space sequencing. But, in *Last Year at Marienbad*, this convention has become replaced with a notion of psychic space as being comprised of more than three dimensions.

Resnais also disrupts notions of predictability and logic by setting up instances, situations, or conversations which disrupt what one might expect in daily life. In fact, elsewhere they might be perceived as sophisticated ridiculing or a series of non sequiturs, but here they contribute to the nightmarish ambience of *Marienbad*.

Why are the members of the party at the hotel, and why do they remain throughout the film elegantly attired in formal evening dress, and dance as if marionettes to the music of the fairground? Why does the camera angle shift perspective so it is unclear who is saying what and to whom? And why is the dialogue out of sequence, as, for example, 'In the summer of 1929, it froze for a week', or 'Have you been here long? No, but I've been here before', or the response to X and M's obsessive playing of the game of 'sevens' which occurs throughout, each time seemingly representing the futility of X's search, the paradoxical 'You can win, but I never lose'. And why is it that, although we see a group of musicians playing violins, what we hear is the sound of a church organ? Thus without a chronology of time and an expected sequencing, there is a radical discontinuity between what is heard and what is seen, to the extent that it is unclear whether the scene is 'real' and in the present, whether it is a film, a memory of a past event, whether it is an imagined projection in the future, or whether it is a dream of a nightmare.

Interpretations

There have been many interpretations of *Last Year at Marienbad*, some unnecessarily harsh, but the film critic, Ginette Vincendeau has written a particularly insightful analysis.[60] She firstly rejects

60 Ginette Vincendeau, 'Introduction' on the Optimum Home Entertainment DVD edition of *Last Year at Marienbad*.

those who have commented on its 'cold intellectualism' and points out it is, in fact 'awash with emotion'. This I would agree with; the desperation of X in response to the continuing refusal of A to respond with any sort of compassion to his memories only serves to increase his anxiety. Time and time again, despite his pleading, his behaviour is that of a man fearing for the loss of his sanity.

The film is above all oblique. Its art subliminal, and its appreciation dependent on the realisation that its subtle, ironic (and witty) references allude to a multi-temporal experience. It suggests also that we as the audience are part of the film. We are also its spectacle, being both subject and object, and therefore of necessity collude with its symmetrical logic. It is a film which works primarily with 'absence', demanding of the viewer imagination, engagement, and a capacity to tolerate not knowing. It is this which makes it truly revolutionary since to search for a definitive narrative or meaning within a film that is so profoundly open to many different interpretations is to believe that life is ultimately capable of definition.

Thus there is no 'preferred reading'. It is an allegory of life, here seen as analogous to psychoanalytic work, allusive, intangible and changing. But it is also a film about obsession, ennui, depression, a state of mind which the film captures in the starkness of its images. What this film offers is a profound protest, what Vincendeau called 'the aesthetics of protest', or what the critical theorist might define as the aestheticism of politics. Thus Vincendeau sees the film as 'a fable for the nuclear age', so profound is its challenge to convention, its challenge to classical narrative structure, its challenge to the accepted stability of a point of view, its representation of the instability of characterisation, and, finally, by the absence, the refusal, of a plot.

Placed within the context of Resnais' other films, one sees again the director's preoccupation with trauma, denial and memories which are lost. It can therefore be interpreted as a critique of apathy, complacency, indifference, and of forgetting. By confronting the rituals of conformity and by questioning who or what represents the 'real', it overturns certainties associated with privilege, here that of class.

Epilogue

'The Past is Never Dead. It's Not Even Past' [61]
Arbours. The Crisis Centre. North London
May 2012

He'd always been a late riser. Today was no different. He had a routine. First tea, then he'd unlock the French windows and if the weather was good enough, step out onto the patio. Finally, he'd take a long, slow, drag on his cigarette. It wouldn't be his last, but it would be his best. He knew he shouldn't smoke. He had a cough. The cough was worse in the winter, but he wasn't planning to give up nicotine. It wasn't the right time. Not now it wasn't.

The sun was already high in the sky. The roofs of the tightly packed Victorian houses surrounding the garden reflected the morning glow. It was quiet, so quiet. The wooden and beautifully designed Scandinavian unit with the central atrium stood in deep shadow at the end of the garden. Designed for reflection, for solitude, for creativity, for time out, he had loved that place. Everybody loved that place but it hadn't always been a tranquil retreat. It had weathered the storms of life: the dramas, the anger, the bitterness, the rage, the hostility, the envy, the hate, and their opposites; the

---

61 William Faulkner from *Requiem for a Nun*. Random House, 1951.

compassion, the forgiveness, the understanding, the love and the affection. A witness to all human life, it now stood, forlorn, silent, abandoned.

Yesterday he'd read through the government document, the latest, written no doubt by a team of civil servants, probably Oxbridge educated, under the direction of the vaguely interested old Etonian Government Minister, whose sole experience of mental health was an elderly aunt suffering with mild dementia. The document was one of 'intent', what the government planned to do, but actually he knew, like everyone else working in the field of mental health, little if any of the recommendations would be implemented. It was merely a smoke screen and a pacifier to all those who, with passion and commitment had presented their case to the relevant Government Committee.

The beginning of the end was apparent years ago: if you wanted to put some date on it there were signs from the last century, the years of Thatcherism, but 2008 was more precise. That was the year of the financial crash. Originating in the States it swept through the financial institutions of the West, including and especially in the City of London, an epicentre for financing global trade. The City had been one of the first to experience the collapse of the markets. The fault? The unregulated banking system, aided and abetted by various others, the venture capitalists, who exploited the chance of a quick buck with little regard for the consequences. The consequences were a dramatic deterioration in the UK economy at both national and local level, which gave a new meaning to the naïve belief in the 'trickledown effect'. And if anyone still hadn't quite grasped the interconnectedness of the individual with the financial groups and institutions of a larger society, the evidence was now there for all to see. The impact was to last for decades.

In one way or another, the money lost had to be recouped and the services for the mentally ill were first in line for cuts. As far as the administration of Arbours went, the regulations began from that time on. From the sublime to the ridiculous, the regulatory grip increased with the passing of each year. Demands came initially from the central government and from there filtered through to the local authorities. The requests for statistical evidence that psychotherapy worked, the refusal to sponsor potential guests for the Crisis Centre, the withholding of some parts of the budget on the grounds that particular work must be undertaken, the insistence on the correct temperature of the tap water, the necessity for training staff in first aid or developing procedures in the case of fire. Some were reasonable requests, some not so, but to implement them required time and resources which distracted from the daily work of psychotherapy.

Many argued control, regulation was not the Arbours way. The organisation had survived very successfully without the tight controls of the bureaucrat. So why should the failures of a financial system based on gambling with other people's money impact upon the work of a psychotherapist? Psychotherapists worked with a different narrative: they challenge the status quo, consider the meaning of an individual's history, and make conscious the unconscious. A philosophical if not a personally political stance which had worked, but an approach that was considered naïve, and moreover anathema to the serving members of the present government.

The gap between a society based increasingly on the monetary values of profit and not much else, now lay in stark contrast to the humanitarianism of organisations such as Arbours. Following 2008, the 'Age of Austerity' was given a new and cruel impetus. Services for the emotionally troubled were seen as irrelevant in the drive for profit and subjected to a less than sympathetic scrutiny. Such ways didn't register on the flickering computer screens within the City of London.

He took another drag from his cigarette and exhaling the smoke watched it rise, hang briefly like a miniature cloud above his head, before disappearing into the still morning air. He sighed, life, all too much; but the mornings were good. The solitude, being alone with his thoughts, the quiet of the day, meant he could do things in his own time … Sudden, shrill, repetitive, a noise like a laser, it cut through his mind and the still, morning air. He squeezed the glowing end of the cigarette between his two fingers, and flicking the stub into the nearest garden border, headed back to the kitchen. As he reached for the phone … it stopped. Whoever it was would ring again, and if they didn't, it couldn't be that important. He glanced at his watch, two hours to go before his therapy session. He sighed.

He eyeballed the house cat, the Arbours cat, the fat, ginger cat. Sitting on the kitchen table. It stared back at him impassively. Over the years, everyone had tried to train it, to keep it off the table, but it always jumped back. It was sitting there now, defiantly waiting to be fed. He opened the cupboard door. The cat jumped off the table and wrapping itself round his legs, purred loudly.

There was no cat food. He'd forgotten. He stared at the solitary packet of instant porridge. Would that do? He shoved some porridge oats with milk into a saucepan, heated and stirred it until it thickened, ran cold water over it, waited five minutes for it to cool, then placed the still warm dollops into a bowl on the floor. He waited. He watched. The cat was not impressed. After a momentary sniff, it walked off, its tail held high in the air. It evidently didn't like porridge, but it continued purring, until faced with the reality of a non-existent breakfast, its meowing increased in volume to a crescendo. He'd had enough. He wanted to be on his own, not catering to this fucking cat.

He picked up the cat, noting how fat and heavy it was, and carrying it outside dumped it at the bottom of the garden just by the compost heap. There were often mice there. It could catch one. It needed to lose weight anyway. Returning to the kitchen, he locked the door, drew the curtains, put the lights on and sat down. He was reaching for his second cigarette, just as he heard the front door slammed. Lisa. It could only be Lisa. He waited.

There was a short pause as she stopped in the hall to check over the post. Always full of energy and compassion, over the years they'd worked and supported each other with some of the most difficult guests. Upbeat as ever, she burst into the kitchen.

'Hiya Si … What the hell are you doing sitting in the dark, with the curtains drawn … and why are the lights on?'

He gave her a world-weary look, 'It's the cat. It's pissing me off, it's invasive, it's in my space. I need a break. I've put it outside.'

'Maybe it wants feeding.'

'Yeah. I know. I know it wants feeding. It made that obvious.'

'Well, feed it then'

'I haven't got the right fucking food. It rejected the porridge … didn't like it … ever noticed that cat's eyes?'

Lisa shrugged, 'No … what about them?'

'They give me the creeps, like they're devil eyes, green, cold, empty, black slanting pupils, but no expression. Staring … as if I've done something wrong … as if it's about to attack.'

'Attack … But you forgot his food, that's all.'

'His … it's an it, but thanks, that makes me feel a whole lot better … not. That cat … it's a persecuting object, it probably inspired Melanie Klein … that's a joke, by the way.'

Lisa was silent for a moment, then, 'How can a cat persecute you? The cat isn't human … Is it? It's an animal.'

'No, it isn't human, but right now it feels to me as if it is … for fuck's sake give me a break.'

Lisa ignored this, walked across to the French windows. 'I want some light in the room, so if you don't mind … ?' She pulled back the floor length curtains, snapped off the light and walked across to the kettle. 'Coffee?'

'Nope. Not coffee, tea, I'm a tea drinker. You should know that by now.'

Lisa didn't reply and silently prepared the drinks. She placed the tea under his nose, and took a seat at the end of the table and looked at him intently. 'Do you remember that guest, the one who left the tap running all night so it flooded everywhere, and the one who put loads of salt in the rhubarb crumble; by mistake, she said.'

'Alison? You mean Alison? The one who tried to poison us?'

'That's the one.'

'What about her?'

'Well, you're like her. You have a similar outlook.' He didn't answer. 'Are you with me?'

'No I'm not with you. I have no idea what you're talking about … she was here … years ago.'

'She was, but she had a thing about animals. She talked about him, the Arbours cat, the whole time. It was never herself that was angry or hungry or didn't like someone; it was the cat. Now do you remember?'

'Ah yes … there was a technical term, Joe told me, anthropomorphise, when you give human qualities to an animal. I get it. I get your point.' He stood up. 'I have my therapy session this morning …' He wandered over to the window and stared out, 'and I'm not about to poison you with salt, but sometimes … it's not so much about murderous intent.' He turned round to look at her. 'I feel mega pissed off this morning … It's like watching someone you love, slowly die.'

There was a long pause, then he said, 'You know what I had to do yesterday? I had to burn the records of the guests who'd stayed here, for confidential reasons … I started reading them, I remember some of them … the ones really difficult, the challenging ones, I remember them the best.'

Lisa sat down and looked at him straight in the eye, 'Some of them, yes, I remember them even after all these years. They made so many demands on us … and they wanted to be sorted … they were desperate, don't you think?'

'It's not so straightforward as that. On the one hand, it was like we were idealised and romanticised, as if we were 'sorted' but then if we got something wrong, we became the devil incarnate.'

Lisa stared into her coffee, then looking straight ahead, she said, 'Yeah. The Crisis Centre … and Joe, we're all going to miss him and the Crisis Centre … but we can do nothing, and in the final analysis …' She sighed. 'I suppose everything has to come to an end.'

'Sometimes, regardless of what they want is …' He paused and stared intensely at his cigarette, leaving his sentence unfinished.

'Understanding?'

'They wanted more. More than that. They wanted our soul … That's how I feel.'

'Maybe they did, but we can't or couldn't give them that, or perhaps we try, and that's why we remember them, because they carry something of ourselves within themselves, and that feels like a loss … our loss, and with that comes …'

She didn't finish. Simon cut her off mid-sentence.

'Last night I … my insomnia, it's back. I hardly fucking slept.'

Lisa looked intently at him. 'It is difficult … it's difficult, I recognise that, especially as you're the 'last man standing' as far as the Crisis Centre goes.'

'Last man standing … true … but the reality is, like I say, all of us, who worked over the years in the Crisis Centre, we're all going to miss it.'

Lisa stood up, and leaning against the sink, watched as he ground his cigarette into a saucer. 'Who are you killing off?'

'What the fuck are you talking about now?' He stared at her.

'You're angry, in a foul mood today, stop swearing, Si' … I'm watching how you're grinding that cigarette. It's violent.'

'What about it?'

'I've said … who are you killing off?'

'I'm not answering that.'

'I think you know.' She began washing out her mug, 'I have to go now. Just came to check the post, but did you say … yes, do you have therapy this morning?'

'Yep.'

Lisa smiled, 'Well, good … have a good one.'

His therapist worked in what had once been the attic at the top of the house. As he climbed the stairs he reflected on the number of times over the years he'd seen him. Four times a week for five years added up, but he rated him and he'd come with Joe's recommendation, and it couldn't get better than that. He loved the 'look' of his consulting room. The white walls, the abstract prints, the stripped floorboards, the two chairs placed diagonally angled, a small writing table under a floor lamp. There must be a 'go-to' design book for therapists' rooms. They all shared a similar ambience of acceptance, restraint, and peace. A bit like a monk's cell. Didn't always work but that was the aim.

His therapist was also a psychiatrist, and like anyone working at Arbours, knew from the inside how limited an analytic interpretation could be. Sometimes a guest, as with the residents in the communities, needed managing, not an interpretation, and at such times when therapists got it wrong and could feel as if metaphorically they'd been put through a compulsory hot wash followed by a fast spin, leaving them dazed, confused and disorientated. When all a patient wanted was a strong, compassionate silence and understanding. He felt like that this morning, but you couldn't prepare for a session, it just didn't work like that. The therapy of silence … in the right time, and in the right place, a rare commodity, of particular value to him … Maybe that's what he needed this morning. Silence. Just silence.

He'd reached the top of the stairs and saw Dr Campbell's door was already partly open. He was sitting in his usual chair.

He gave Simon a quick nod of recognition. This was always accompanied by a mutual but brief, intense scrutiny, each observing what mood the other might be experiencing. Although Simon was aware that if his therapist had moods, he'd keep them to himself.

For five minutes, he sat trying to orientate himself. He wasn't quite sure where to start until he realised, it was going to be about the Crisis Centre. This was going to be painful. It would bring back the difficulties of his first days at the Crisis Centre. Lisa's comment, about being the last man standing was spot on. From the start of his time at the Crisis Centre, that's how he'd felt. Total responsibility. In fact, it was the story of his life.

At that point and as if from a distance, he heard Dr Campbell ask, 'Where are your thoughts?'

He didn't respond, not straight away. He'd almost forgotten he was there, sitting with him in the same room. He shrugged, 'Not sure where I am today …' There was a long silence.

'Can you say a little more?'

'I didn't sleep well last night ... thinking, you know, this and that, the people ... from the past. It's heavy'.

'Is or was?'

'Right now, it's heavy, burning those papers. At the Crisis Centre. It's final ... it's finished.'

'And before?'

'What do you mean?'

'You mentioned the past, people from the past. We've talked before about your past. What's being triggered? Something is, we need to make a connection.'

'I was talking about today, things that need doing, stuff I have to do, take responsibility for ... to be honest. It feels like I've been left holding the baby. I wasn't asked. I don't want to do it. It would be easy to just walk away.'

'Maybe so, but something is stopping you. What or who is stopping you?'

'I don't know ... I feel responsible.'

There was another long silence.

'It's difficult for you today.'

'It is difficult. I thought I'd dealt with that, but I haven't. I don't want it back again.'

Memories. Nobody listened. Nobody. I was just left with it all. It feels too much ... History repeats itself, the first time a tragedy, the second time a farce. Do you know that one?' Dr Campbell remained silent, and made no comment. Simon stood up, walked across to the window, looked out, then paused, before saying, 'The cherry blossom has finished.'

He said it without thinking, its meaning escaped him, but apparently not his therapist. He didn't respond, not immediately, but his question 'So what do you make of that?' provoked a memory. Brought it all back.

The image of his mother, lying in her bedroom. Thin, painfully thin, her complexion yellow, her skin like paper, her hair pulled back from her face, her eyes huge as she watched him cross the floor towards her. 'Did you ask him?'

'Yes, I asked him.'

'Did you say I was ill?'

'Yes, I did'

'What did he say?'

'Nothing. He said nothing.'

'Did you bring me … you know what I like.'

Simon turned to face him. 'I asked him to come, and the rest of them. Some came and some didn't so it was just me. That's what …' he didn't finish his sentence and stared across the room.

'You were left with?'

'Yes. It's too much, too much responsibility.'

'Holding the baby.'

'Baby? Did I say that?'

'You did, but I'm wondering who was the baby.'

'It's just a metaphor.'

'But we both know that a metaphor isn't random. It has meaning. What comes to mind, when you think of a baby?'

'Hard to say … how would I know?.'

'We're in two different time frames now. Past and present. Maybe we can start with the baby. The one in the past. How would you describe your baby?'

'I haven't a baby …'

'I know that, but we're in another realm—of responsibility but not knowing.'

'Do you mean I've blocked it off … in the unconscious?'

'Precisely, but what's that? It's not simply a word. Give me some thoughts.'

A long silence, before he spoke, then, 'She has no regard for me, incessantly demanding, nothing pleases her, she is all want, drink and more drink, do this, do that, will I get this, did I remember that, she thinks there's something wrong with me, she asks what I think of her, is she pretty, does she still look young, will I go with her to see her friends, I'm not like other children, they're successful, well off, they look after their mothers … on and on and on.' A long pause … 'I hate her. She wanted my soul.'

He begins pacing round the room.

Dr Campbell takes time before he speaks. His voice is calm, containing. 'You see the connection?'

'No, what connection? … Maybe. Yes, I think so … I'm not sure. I don't know'

'You love her, but you feel responsible, it's too much, you've been left holding the baby. Why? Because a certain and important person, never referred to, is invisible, it's as if he doesn't exist, he's disappeared, leaving you with this monstrous baby. Who was he? Or who is he?'

'You mean my father, is that who you mean? He left me with her. Just disappeared. So I had to look after her and I didn't want to do that. She repulsed me … the missing father. My father. In at the beginning but not the end.'

'Tell me how you feel.'

Simon stops and standing directly facing Dr Campbell, he says, 'You really want to know? Well, I'll tell you. Fucking awful. I feel betrayed, exploited, angry, powerless and that's just the beginning … He can go fuck himself for all I care. They're all the fucking same and I've had enough'

Dr Campbell is silent, then he speaks, 'The gap, the gap of time, the presence of the past, it needs understanding. Here it's about the significance for you of your absent father … then and now, but still … still you feel it as intensely as you did all those years ago. For years the Crisis Centre has been your life, it filled a gap, and it's coming to an end. You feel abandoned, bereft, left alone with a responsibility just like before, and it feels too great a burden to carry. Its true significance … the intensity of your loss now, today can only be fully understood in terms of the power of your past, your hopes, and the disappointments of your own past.'

Simon sighed, and leaning forward with his elbows on his knees, stared at the floor intensely, before pulling himself up out of the chair to leave, 'It's time to go. But I get it …'

'What do you get?'

'The cherry blossom has fallen, that's what I said, didn't I? … It all makes sense now.'

'William Faulkner, the American writer, said once, "The past is never dead. It's not even past."'

Simon walked again to the window and stood looking out, before turning towards Dr Campbell.

'Thank you.'

Dr Campbell stood up. 'But the phrase, Faulkner's words, retains some ambiguity … Wednesday, as usual. We'll continue.'

'Ambiguity? What do you mean?'

'We have choices. The past doesn't have to control the present.'

'Maybe not … but …'

'We have time.'

'But do we? Do we? Who cares? Who will listen now to those who need to be heard and understood?'

Biographies

Marguerite Valentine established with others, one of the first Refuges for women and children subjected to domestic violence. Subsequently qualifying for an M.A in Social Work at Warwick University, she later worked in Child Protection and Long Term Care of Children. Her Ph.D. in Critical Theory followed through her interest in the relationship between the personal and the sociological, and informed her decision to train with the Arbours Association. For some years she represented Arbours on the *British Journal of Psychotherapy*'s Editorial Board. She is the author of various clinical papers on psychoanalytic issues, film analysis, and also three novels.

Susan Budnick trained at the Arbours Association and at the Couples and Family Institute of New England, Boston, MA. Since 2004 she has worked as a Psychoanalyst in the US. She is currently a member of the National Ass. for the advancement of Psychoaalysis and a Licensed Psychoanalyst and Couples Therapist. In 2015 she spoke at the Esalen Conference held in California about R. D. Laing and the work of the Arbours Therapeutic Communities .

Diana Turner qualified as a Social Worker in 1983. She always worked in Child Care, finally working as a County Reviewing Officer for Children with Disabilities. She subsequently qualified as a Counsellor, setting up a Staff Counselling Service for a local health authority, and after training as a Psychoaalytic Psychotherapist with the Arbours Association, for many years worked both in the NHS and in private practice.

Steve Baker initially worked as an Addiction Counsellor in the Voluntary Sector before moving to the NHS and completing a Psychodynamic Counselling course. His developing interest in psychoanalysis and psycho-social thinking led to his training as a Psychoanalytic Psychotherapist with Arbours. For some years he was employed by Arbours in the Crisis Centre as a Residential Psychotherapist. He has a successful private practice in central London.

Acknowledgements

As with a therapy session, I initially thought of this book as an experience and its writing as both therapeutic and challenging. Various issues cropped up along the way, but I was helped through and round such obstacles, by the following colleagues and friends. I am eternally grateful for their assistance and unfailing support.

Steve Baker, who was insightfully thoughtful and helpful at every stage, and who contributed to the section on the Crisis Centre, Diana Turner who was prepared to listen and freely offer her valuable insights. She wrote a piece on the Community. Susan Budnick with whom I shared many interesting discussions before she moved back to the States. She also contributed a section. Andy Aires and Judith Kettle whose professional background in Social Work and continuing interest in my 'project' was much appreciated.

Dr Morton Schatzman, a founding member of the Arbours Associations along with Dr Joseph Berke. Dr Berke sadly has since died two years ago but his charismatic quirkiness will not be forgotten. Dr Schatzman gave me many leads re the origins of radical psychotherapy and his reference to the Faulkner quotation, was an unexpected gift. I very much appreciated his support and enthusiasm.

Dr Andrea Sabbadini who shares a similar passion with myself in psychoanalytically informed films and whose comments on the clinical use of film narrative were extremely helpful.

Thanks also for the psychic and intellectual contributions of Dr Robin Gordon Brown and Dr Richard Carvalho who both read through several versions of certain chapters without complaint.

Andrew Lockett for his first class copy editing, Richard Grove for his computing skills and Jill Adams whose understanding of Word was phenomenal. Finally, to my two sons, Marcus, whose laconic and humorous reflections on life have always stood me in good stead, and Justin, whose legally trained incisive mind refreshingly grounded my occasional flights of fantasy.

Covers designed by Marguerite Valentine and Richard Grove. Photograph by Christophe Dutour on Unsplash.

Printed in Great Britain
by Amazon